AF413211

ANIMALS
500
QUESTIONS
AND ANSWERS

Clare Hibbert

ARCTURUS

This edition published in 2026 by Arcturus Publishing Limited
26/27 Bickels Yard, 151–153 Bermondsey Street,
London SE1 3HA

Author: Clare Hibbert
Illustrator: Jake McDonald
Editors: William Potter and Lydia Halliday
Designer : Sarah Fountain
Editorial Manager: Joe Harris
Managing Designer: Georgina Wood

ISBN: 978-1-3988-6833-5
CH012490NT
Supplier 29, Date 0326, PI 00010550

Printed in China

INTRODUCTION

If you had a chance to ask an animal expert any question, what would you ask?

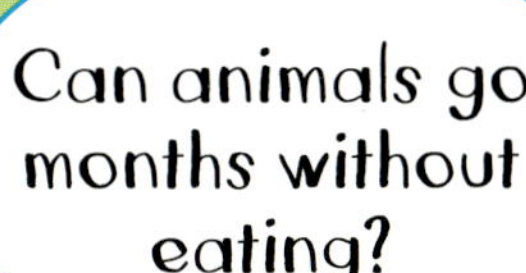

In this book, you'll find the answers to hundreds of clever questions about the animal kingdom, and discover creatures that do the most surprising things.

You'll visit jungles, deserts, rain forests, the poles, and the deepest parts of the ocean. So, what are you waiting for? Turn the page!

WHAT IS THE BIGGEST ANIMAL EVER?

The blue whale is the biggest animal to have ever lived on Earth. It can grow up to 33.5 m (110 ft)—as long as 18 scuba divers end to end.

How heavy is blue whale's heart?

A blue whale's heart weighs 180 kg (400 lb)—as heavy as a lion.

How can it float?

A blue whale reaches 181 tonnes (200 tons)—the same as 28 African elephants. Its tongue alone weighs as much as one elephant, but water supports the whale's weight.

How long do blue whales live for?

Blue whales live for up to 90 years.

Are blue whales noisy?

Blue whales are one of the loudest animals. Their call measures 188 decibels.

WHAT IS THE LIGHTEST MAMMAL?

At just 1.8 g (0.06 oz), the tiny Etruscan shrew is the world's lightest mammal—lighter than a sugar lump. Its body is just 4 cm (1.6 in) long!

What is its heart rate?

Small mammals often have fast heart rates, and the Etruscan shrew is no different. Its heart beats up to 1,500 times a minute—more than ten times faster than yours!

Does the shrew eat tiny meals?

The Etruscan shrew eats almost twice its own body weight in worms and grubs every day!

Is there a smaller mammal?

The bumblebee bat weighs 0.2 g (0.01 oz) more than an Etruscan shrew, but its skull is a fraction smaller.

DOES AN OSTRICH BURY ITS HEAD IN THE SAND?

There's a saying that the ostrich buries its head, meaning it ignores danger. In fact, the world's biggest bird usually runs from any threat.

Is the ostrich the biggest bird ever?

Weighing up to 275 kg (600 lb), the elephant bird was even bigger than the ostrich. It lived on Madagascar until 500 years ago.

Do ostriches have other escape plans?

If running is not an option, an ostrich throws itself on the ground. Its head and neck blend in with the sand, but its big body is still visible!

Can ostriches fly?

Ostriches are too heavy to fly. Males can weigh up to 156 kg (346 lb)—as much as a sumo wrestler.

WHAT IS THE SMALLEST BIRD?

The smallest bird is the tiny bee hummingbird. At just 5 cm (2 in) long, it is not much bigger than a bee.

How fast do hummingbirds flap their wings?

Bee hummingbirds beat their wings around 80 times a second—too fast for the human eye to see. When a male is showing off to attract a mate, he can flap his wings even faster—up to 200 times per second!

Where does the bee hummingbird live?

It lives in swamps and forests in Cuba.

What does a bee hummingbird eat?

Bee hummingbirds feed on nectar and insects. In a typical day, one bird can visit up to 1,500 flowers.

WHAT ARE PRIMATES?

The primate family includes apes, monkeys, lemurs, and tarsiers.

Mandrill

The male mandrill has a blue and red face and a pink bottom. It is the biggest monkey and lives in African rain forests.

chimpanzee

Ape or monkey?

Monkeys have tails while apes do not. Chimpanzees, gorillas, orangutans, gibbons, and humans are all apes!

Which ape is most like us?

Chimpanzees are our closest animal relatives. We share more than 98% of our DNA with them!

Golden lion tamarin

The endangered golden lion tamarin is named for its lionlike mane. It lives in Brazil.

Which primate has a huge nose?

The male proboscis monkey has an enormous nose. It can grow as long as 10.2 cm (4 in)!

Proboscis monkey

Which baby takes its mama for a ride?

A ring-tailed lemur baby clings to its mother's chest for the first two weeks of life. Then it rides on her back!

Ring-tailed lemurs

Where do orangutans live?

Orangutans are the only large apes in Asia. They live on the islands of Borneo and Sumatra and are the biggest tree-dwelling mammals.

Orangutan

What are the largest primates?

Gorillas are the largest primates. They spend most of their time on the ground, but sleep in nests in the trees.

Gorilla

How long are orangutan arms?

Orangutans are the kings of the swingers! Their arms can stretch 2 m (7 ft) fingertip to fingertip.

DO INSECTS HAVE SKELETONS?

No, instead they have a tough outer case called an exoskeleton.

Does the exoskeleton grow?

As an insect grows, it becomes too big for its exoskeleton—but that's not a problem! It wriggles out of the old case and leaves it behind. There's a shiny new exoskeleton underneath.

Do all insects come in three parts?

Insects include beetles, bugs, flies, bees, butterflies, and grasshoppers. In their adult form, they all have three pairs of legs and three parts to their body. Woodlice have too many legs to be insects, but they do have exoskeletons.

Are insects anthropods?

Yes. Arthropods live on land, in fresh water, and in the sea. They all have jointed legs and a tough exoskeleton.

ARE MOST ANIMALS SPINELESS?

Animals that don't have spines or other inside bones are called invertebrates. More than 97% of all the animals on Earth are invertebrates!

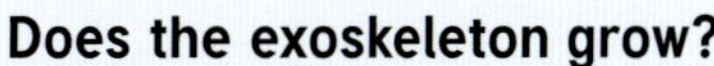

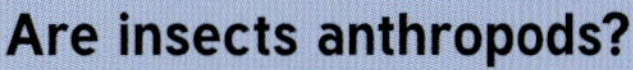

Which animals are invertebrates?
There are six groups of invertebrates:

- arthropods (insects, spiders, and crustaceans)
- jellyfish, corals, and sea anemones
- starfish, sea cucumbers, and sea urchins
- mollusks (snails, slugs, squid, and octopuses)
- segmented worms
- sponges

Spider

Butterfly

Snail

What is the biggest arthropod?

The biggest arthropod is the Japanese crab, with an arm span of 3.8 m (12.5 ft). Arthropods live on land, in fresh water, and in the sea. They all have jointed legs and a tough exoskeleton.

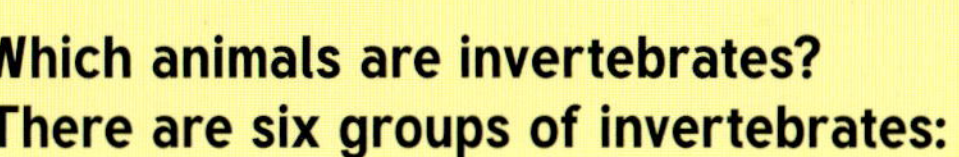

Starfish

Octopus

Sea urchin

Fly

Centipede

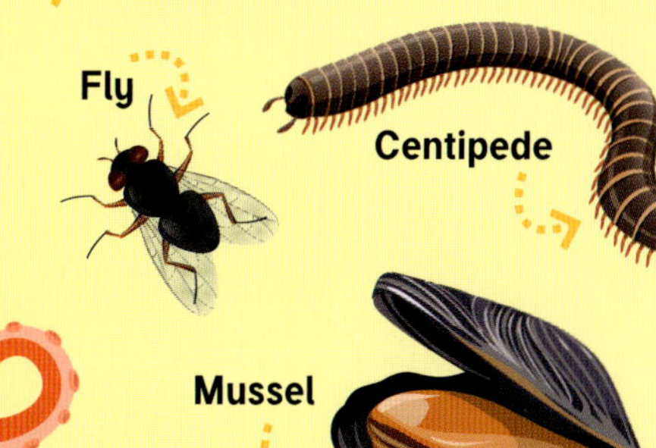

Mussel

WHICH BIRD HAS THE WIDEST WINGSPAN?

With wings outstretched, an albatross can easily cover the length of your car. Its whopping wingspan of 3.5 m (11 ft) allows it to soar over the seas.

Does the albatross fly without flapping?

The albatross saves energy by hardly ever flapping its wings. It drifts down toward the sea, then faces into the wind to be blown skyward again.

Albatross

Is the albatross the largest ever flyer?

Some past flyers were even larger than the albatross. *Quetzalcoatlus*, a large pterosaur, had a wingspan of about 11 m (36 ft).

***Quetzalcoatlus*, a large pterosaur**

HOW MANY BONES ARE IN A GIRAFFE'S NECK?

The giraffe has the longest neck in the animal kingdom, at around 1.8 m (6 ft) long. However, just seven neck bones support its length.

Do giraffes have neck fights?

Male giraffes bash each other's necks when they want to impress a female.

Giraffe

Do giraffes have more neck bones than humans?

No. Almost every mammal—from mice to giraffes and anteaters to humans—has seven neck bones. Each giraffe neck bone is around 25.4 cm (10 in) long.

Do any animals have more bones?

Birds have more neck bones than many other animals—up to 25 of them.

Mouse

HOW MANY ARMS DO STARFISH HAVE?

The best-known starfish have five arms, but some have up to 40. "Sea stars" is a better name than "starfish," because these weird and wonderful creatures are definitely not fish!

Do sea stars have eyes?

The sea star has a simple eye at the end of each arm. It can't see well, but its limited vision helps keep it close to home.

How many different sea stars are there?

There are around 2,000 different species of sea star and they live all over the world. Their average life span is about 35 years!

DO MILLIPEDES HAVE A THOUSAND LEGS?

Their name means "1,000 feet," but most millipedes have between 80 and 400 legs. They have two pairs per body segment, and they grow new segments (and legs!) as they age.

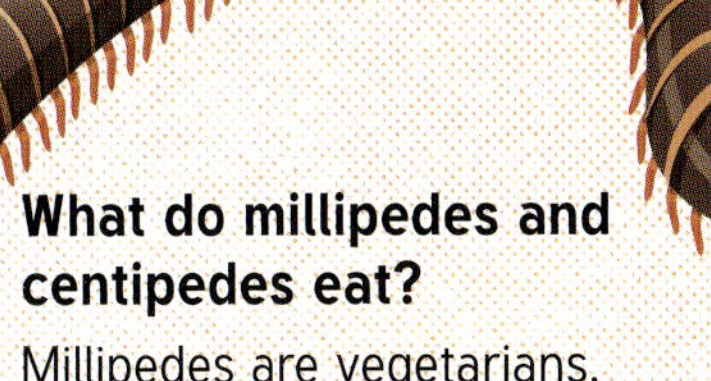

What do millipedes and centipedes eat?

Millipedes are vegetarians, but their cousins, the centipedes, are hunters.

How many legs do centipedes have?

"Centipede" means "100 legs," but they can have between 30 and 350 legs. Their bodies are flatter than millipedes'.

Which millipede has the most legs?

One rare millipede, from California, has up to 750 legs! They must be very tiny because the critter's body is only 3 cm (1 in) long.

DOES A PYTHON CHEW?

A snake doesn't chew its food—it swallows it whole! It stretches its jaw to accommodate super-sized meals, such as a pig, antelope, or person!

How long do pythons grow?

Burmese pythons grow up to 7 m (23 ft) long.

How big a meal can a python swallow?

In 2015, scientists X-rayed a python that had eaten an alligator. It took three days to break down the soft tissue. After a week it had digested the skeleton and skin.

What makes the python's jaw so special?

1. It isn't stuck firmly to the skull.
2. It has two pieces, joined by stretchy ligament, and the two halves can open apart.

WHY ARE HUMMINGBIRD BEAKS SO LONG?

A hummingbird's long, pointy beak looks like a drinking straw. The bird seems to slurp nectar through it.

How much do hummingbirds eat?

Hummingbirds eat half of their body weight in sugar every day!

Do hummingbirds suck up food?

The hummingbird doesn't really suck up sugary nectar—it laps it. Inside the beak, its fringed, forked tongue unfurls to grab nectar, then curls up again to carry it into the bird's mouth!

How long can their beaks grow?

The sword-billed hummingbird has a beak longer than its body. Its beak can be 10 cm (4 in) long.

DO RODENT TEETH KEEP ON GROWING?

To stop themselves from having longer fangs than Dracula, rodents must wear down their incisor teeth with constant gnawing. Their name comes from the Latin word *rodere*, "to gnaw!"

Chipmunk

red squirrel

mouse

What is the biggest rodent?

Rodents include rats, chipmunks, squirrels, and beavers. The largest is the capybara, which looks like a giant guinea pig. It grows up to 1.3 m (4.4 ft) long.

Capybara

And the smallest?

The smallest rodents, the pygmy jerboa and the pygmy mouse, are around 5 cm (2 in) long, excluding their tails.

Are rabbits rodents?

Rabbits, hares, and pikas aren't rodents, but they are close cousins. Their incisor teeth never stop growing either!

Arctic hare

DO ALL ELEPHANTS HAVE TUSKS?

All African elephants have tusks, but only some Asian males have them. Tusks are extra-long incisor teeth.

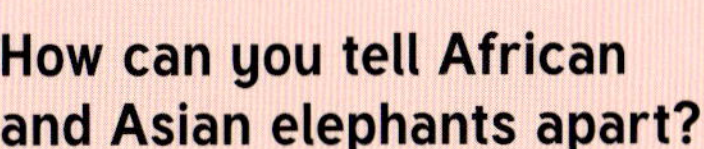
Asian elephant

What are tusks used for?

Elephants use their tusks to battle enemies, dig, and forage. Tusks never stop growing and can be 3.5 m (11.5 ft) or more.

Which animal had the longest tusks?

The longest mammoth tusks were 4.8 m (16 ft). Mastodons were prehistoric relatives of elephants and mammoths. Their tusks were even larger—nearly 5 m (16.4 ft) long!

How can you tell African and Asian elephants apart?

African elephants have larger ears, shaped like the African continent. Asian elephants have smaller ears.

African elephant

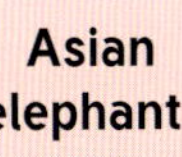
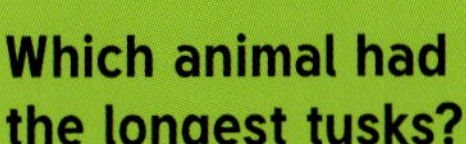
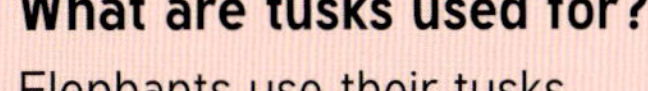

IS A CHAMELEON'S TONGUE LONGER THAN ITS BODY?

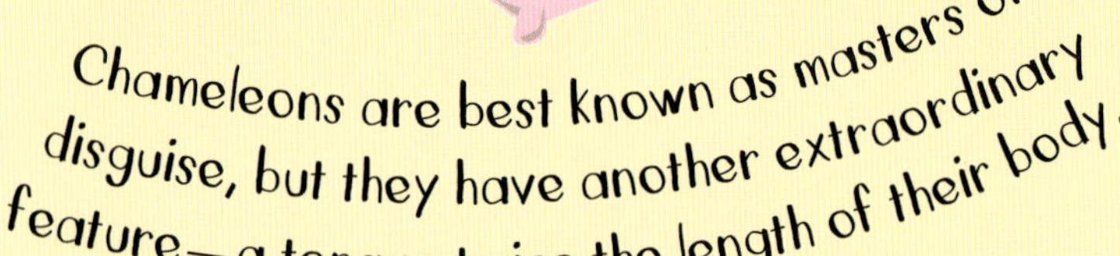

Chameleons are best known as masters of disguise, but they have another extraordinary feature—a tongue twice the length of their body.

How fast is its tongue?

If the chameleon's tongue were a car, it could accelerate from 0 to 96.6 kph (60 mph) in one hundredth of a second.

How do chameleons hunt?

A chameleon sits motionless for hours. When it spots insect prey, it shoots out its long, sticky tongue. The tongue is back in its mouth—along with the meal—too fast for the eye to see!

If your teacher's tongue was twice their body length, it'd be 3-3.6 m (10-12 ft) long!

WHAT IS THE WORLD'S BIGGEST SPIDER?

The Goliath bird-eating spider is the world's biggest spider. It has a 28- cm (11- in) leg span and weighs up to 175 g (6.2 oz).

Do they only eat birds?

Despite their name, Goliath bird-eating spiders mostly eat invertebrates, mice, frogs, and lizards. However, they can take bigger prey, including snakes and birds.

Is there a spider with longer legs?

The giant huntsman spider has a smaller body than the Goliath bird-eater, but longer legs. These help it to run down fast-moving prey, such as cockroaches or other spiders.

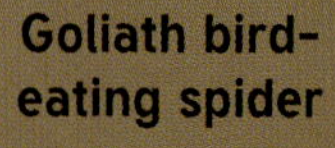
Goliath bird-eating spider

WHICH WHALES DIVE THE DEEPEST?

Sperm whales hold the record for the longest, deepest dives of any mammal.

What is special about deep divers?

Deep-diving mammals have extra helpings of myoglobin in their muscles. It's a special protein that stores oxygen.

What other animals are marine mammals?

Sea otters, sea lions, seals, dolphins, and polar bears are all marine mammals.

How long can they stay underwater?

All marine mammals must come to the surface to breathe air. Sperm whales can stay underwater for as long as an hour-and-a-half and dive to depths of 999.7 m (3,280 ft). They feed on giant squid.

Sperm whale

Harp seal

Do jellyfish have brains?

There are more than 4,000 species of jellyfish, but none have brains!

How does the puffer fish defend itself?

The puffer fish puffs up its body to frighten away predators.

Puffer fish

Jellyfish

What is the smallest jellyfish?

The smallest jellyfish, the Irukandji jellyfish, is only 2.5 cm (0.98 in), but its venom can kill a person.

Eel

Are eels fish?

Yes. There are more than 400 species of eel.

Sea cucumber

Is a sea cucumber a fruit?

No, the sea cucumber is related to sea stars and sea urchins—not the cucumber plant!

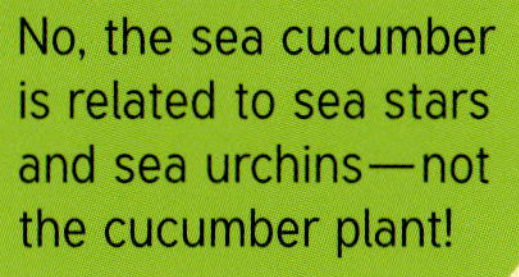

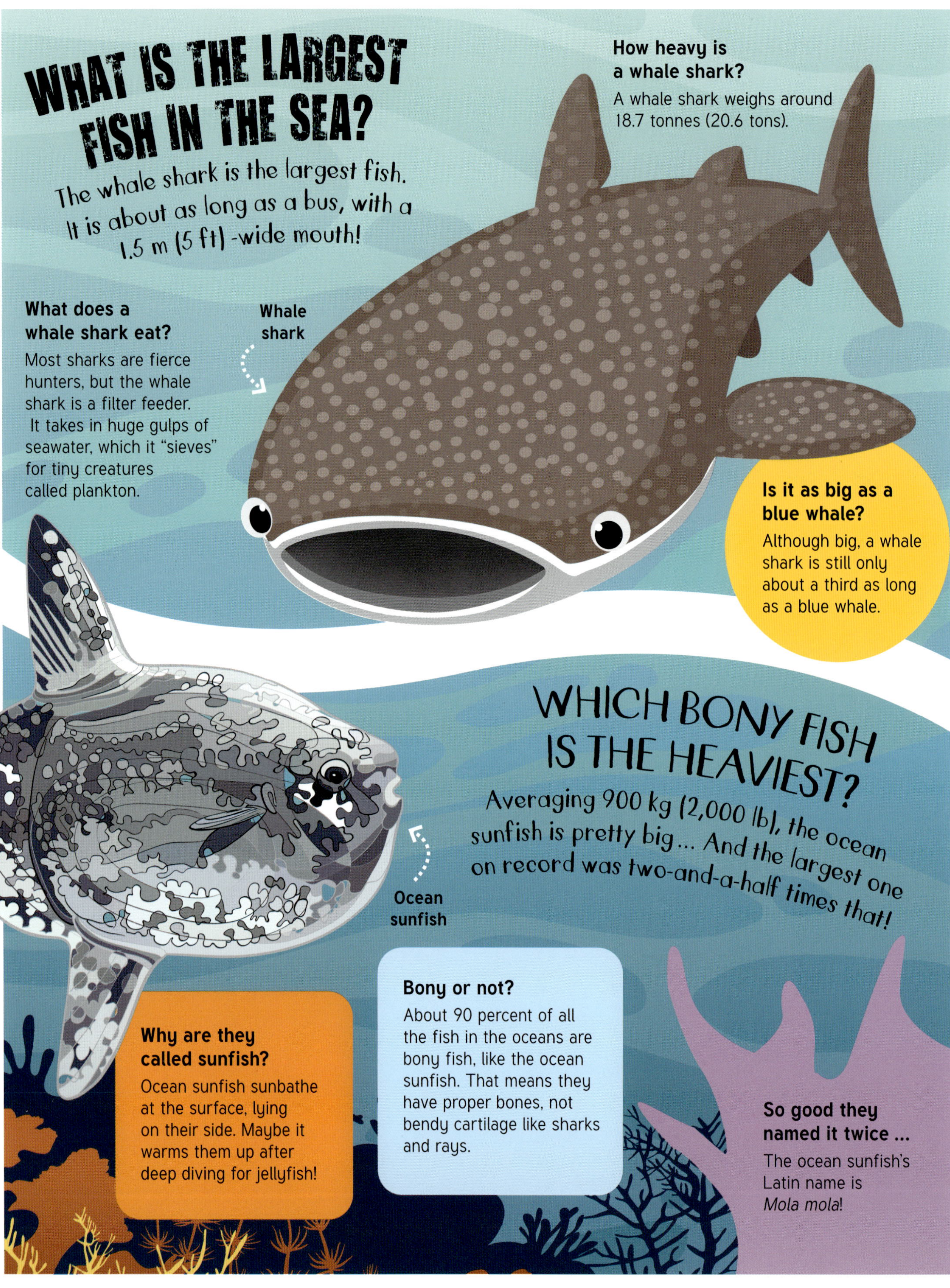

WHAT IS THE LARGEST FISH IN THE SEA?

The whale shark is the largest fish. It is about as long as a bus, with a 1.5 m (5 ft) -wide mouth!

How heavy is a whale shark?

A whale shark weighs around 18.7 tonnes (20.6 tons).

What does a whale shark eat?

Most sharks are fierce hunters, but the whale shark is a filter feeder. It takes in huge gulps of seawater, which it "sieves" for tiny creatures called plankton.

Is it as big as a blue whale?

Although big, a whale shark is still only about a third as long as a blue whale.

WHICH BONY FISH IS THE HEAVIEST?

Averaging 900 kg (2,000 lb), the ocean sunfish is pretty big... And the largest one on record was two-and-a-half times that!

Why are they called sunfish?

Ocean sunfish sunbathe at the surface, lying on their side. Maybe it warms them up after deep diving for jellyfish!

Bony or not?

About 90 percent of all the fish in the oceans are bony fish, like the ocean sunfish. That means they have proper bones, not bendy cartilage like sharks and rays.

So good they named it twice ...

The ocean sunfish's Latin name is *Mola mola!*

WHAT WAS THE FIRST PET?

The first domesticated animal was the dog. Humans tamed the wolf around 30,000 years ago.

Which dog is the tallest?

The Great Dane is the tallest dog breed, standing 76 cm (30 in) at the shoulder.

Which pets talk back?

Budgies, cockatoos, and other parrots make friendly, talkative pets.

How many dogs are kept in the United States?

More than a third of US households have a pet dog.

What is a cockatiel?

The cockatiel is a small kind of cockatoo. It comes from Australia.

Which dog is the smallest?

The Chihuahua is the smallest dog breed. The tiniest stand at less than 10 cm (4 in).

Which pet cat is the largest?

The largest breed of pet cat is the Maine Coon. One record-breaker weighed 15.9 kg (35 lb).

Who first kept goldfish?

The Chinese were the first people to keep pet goldfish.

When was the first cat show?

The first-ever cat show was held in London, UK, in the 1870s.

Which cat is most popular in the US?

The Persian is the most popular cat breed in the US.

HOW LONG DO GIRAFFES SLEEP FOR?

An adult giraffe has just 15 to 30 minutes of sleep in any 24-hour period.

Do lions nap for longer?

Lions, the main predators in the giraffe's grassland home, sleep for 20 hours per day.

Do they have a deep sleep?

No. The giraffe naps for a minute or two at a time, either standing up or lying down. It takes this spindly giant time to get up from the floor, so it snoozes with one eye open, watching for danger.

How do dolphins swim and come up for air, but also sleep?

They shut down one side of their brain at a time, including the eye it controls.

ARE SLOTHS THE SLEEPIEST ANIMALS?

The sloth has such a reputation for snoozing that even its name means "laziness!"

Giant armadillos sleep a lot, too—for as much as 18 hours per day.

Is there a lazier animal?

Sloths sleep for 20 hours a day, but Australia's koala sleeps for 22 hours! Its diet doesn't help. The koala eats only eucalyptus leaves, which take a very long time to digest.

What do koalas eat?

Koalas eat about 1.1 kg (2.5 lb) of eucalyptus a day. The leaves must travel along its 2- m (6.6- ft) gut, which is more than three times the animal's body length!

DO LIZARDS "DROP" THEIR TAILS?

Lizards have a neat trick for distracting predators—they let the end of their tail fall off.

Why would a predator fall for this trick?

The tail wriggles, flips, and tumbles long after it's detached from the body. Hopefully it holds the predator's attention while the lizard makes its getaway.

What happens to the tail?

The tail moves about so much that the predator cannot catch it. When the coast is clear, the lizard may come back and eat its own tail. Sounds gross? It means the lizard can get back some of the energy it lost. It'll need it to regrow its tail.

What happens when a worm is cut in two?

When an earthworm is cut in two, the half with its head can regrow a new tail.

CAN CREATURES REGROW BODY PARTS?

The axolotl, a kind of salamander, is a champion regenerator. It can replace a tail or leg, and even mend its own heart or brain!

A spiny mouse can completely heal wounds or grow back missing skin in record time!

Can sea stars regrow arms?

A sea star can regrow any arm that breaks off!

Do deer antlers grow back?

A deer can regrow 27 kg (60 lb) of antlers in just three months!

IS SPIDER SILK STRONGER THAN STEEL?

Yes. Bridges aren't built from silk just yet, however...

How do spider silk and steel compare?

Spider silk cannot take quite as much stress as steel before it breaks. But the silk is so much less dense than steel that it wins out. It is five times stronger than the same weight of steel.

Where does spider silk come from?

A spider uses body parts called spinnerets to shape the silk.

Do spiders weave with gold?

Female golden orb spiders produce golden silk.

What is spider silk used for?

Spiders make their silk from proteins. They use it for many jobs, including building webs, protecting eggs, ballooning through the air, and wrapping up their prey like mummies.

Black widow spider

How much is the largest pearl worth?

The record-breaking pearl belonged to a fisherman from the Philippine Islands, who used to touch it for luck. Worth more than $100 million, the pearl had formed inside a giant clam shell.

How are pearls formed?

Oysters, clams, and mussels all produce pearls if grit gets inside their shell. Their body covers the object with thin, pearly layers so it cannot irritate them. Pearls chosen for jewels are often perfectly round.

HOW BIG IS THE LARGEST PEARL?

The biggest known pearl is pillow-sized and weighs as much as an adult labrador retriever.

Are all pearls made by oysters?

Not all pearls are natural. Some are made in factories.

Pearl

WHERE DO SLOTHS HANG OUT?

Sloths are super-cute mammals that live in rain forest trees in Central and South America.

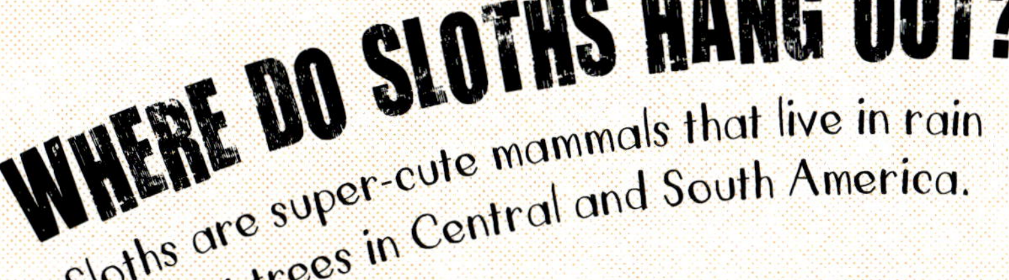

Do sloths ever leave the trees?

Sloths come down to the forest floor once a week and stand the right way up to poop and urinate. That doesn't sound like very often, but sloths' digestive systems are slow, too!

Do sloths spend most of their time upside down?

Yes. They appear motionless but are actually moving very, very slowly. Their long, strong claws grip the tree branches.

Sloth

CAN LIZARDS "FLY?"

The Draco lizard has winglike flaps on the sides of its body. It's not capable of powered flight, but it can glide from tree to tree.

Draco lizard

How far can they glide?

All 42 species of *Draco* lizard can glide as far as 60 m (200 ft). Their "wing" membranes are supported on extra-long ribs that stick out from the body. Flying geckos follow a different design—their "wings" are flaps that join their limbs and body.

Flying gecko

Flying frog

Do flying frogs have wings?

No. Flying frogs stay airborne thanks to extra webbing between their toes. They spread them out to catch the air.

Do hippos make sunscreen?

Hippos ooze oily, reddish-orange "sweat" from pores in their skin. It contains chemicals that soak up dangerous ultraviolet (UV) light—the rays that damage skin. The sweat is antibacterial too, so it stops wounds from getting infected.

CAN HIPPOS GET SUNBURNT?

Hippopotamuses live in sub-Saharan Africa. They wallow in rivers all day to keep cool, but they still need protection from the hot sun's dangerous rays.

Do hippos sweat blood?

People used to think that hot hippos sweated blood, but this is just the pigment of their "sweat."

DO WHALES GET SUN TANS?

Blue whales spend their winter vacations in the sunnier seas around Mexico. Their skin reacts to the extra UV light—it produces darker pigments, just like human skin when it tans.

Do whales sunbathe?

Sperm whales spend up to six hours at a time basking at the water's surface. Their skin contains proteins that help it to avoid UV damage.

Do all whales tan?

Fin whales are different. They are naturally darker-skinned than blue whales because they have a pigment called melanin in their skin. The melanin protects against the sun.

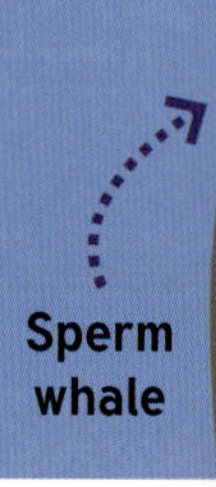

ARE SHEEP SURE-FOOTED?

Wild sheep live on hills and mountains. If they weren't steady on their feet, they'd always be slipping on loose rocks or tripping over cliffs.

Bighorn sheep

Mountain goat

How do sheep survive in the mountains?

Sheep have thick, woolly hair to keep out the cold. They huddle together in flocks for warmth and as a protection against wolves and other mountain predators.

Are wild goats and sheep related?

Yes, but they're not the same. Wild sheep are larger and have thicker horns. Wild goats are native to North America, while wild sheep come from Asia.

WHICH CATTLE NEED LARGE LUNGS?

Yaks are wild cattle from the Himalayas. Extra-large lungs help them to survive in their harsh habitat.

Yak

How common are yaks?

There are more than 12 million domestic yaks, but only around 10,000 wild ones.

Why do yaks need deep breaths?

At high altitudes, the air's thinner and contains less oxygen. Thanks to its big lungs, the yak takes in more air with each breath. It also has an extra-high count of red blood cells—the ones that carry oxygen around the body.

Why do they have a shaggy coat?

Yaks' thick coats help them to survive temperatures as low as -40 °C (-40 °F). In winter, yaks eat snow to keep themselves hydrated.

WHAT WERE THE FIRST FARM ANIMALS?

Sheep and goats were the first animals tamed to be a source of food, around 11,000 years ago.

Dog

Why were dogs domesticated?

Early people tamed dogs to help them to hunt and to guard their settlements.

How can you tell how a turkey's feeling?

A turkey's wattle changes shade with its mood.

Turkey

Goat

Do goats have top teeth?

Goats and sheep don't have teeth in their upper jaws.

How tall was the tallest horse?

The tallest, heaviest horse ever known was a Shire horse called Sampson. It weighed 1,524 kg (3,360 lb).

Chicken

Egg

How big can a pig get?

The largest pig, a Poland China called Big Bill, weighed 1,157 kg (2,550 lb).

How many eggs do chickens lay?

Some chickens lay more than 300 eggs a year.

Which is the tiniest chicken?

The smallest chicken is the Serama. It's less than 25 cm (9.8 in) tall.

Rabbit

When were rabbits first domesticated?

French monks were the first to breed rabbits for food, just 1,400 years ago.

DO POLAR BEARS HAVE WHITE SKIN?

No. They may look white, but polar bears actually have clear fur and their skin is black, not white!

How does black skin help?

Black skin protects the polar bear from the sun's strong UV rays, but also helps it soak up maximum heat.

Why do polars bears look white?

Polar bear hair looks white (even though it's clear) for four reasons:

1. Sunlight bounces inside the hollow hairs, creating a glow.
2. Teeny-tiny bumps on the hairs' surfaces scatter the light.
3. The hairs contain proteins called keratin, which are white.
4. Salt from the ocean may coat the hairs, too.

DO BEARS SLEEP ALL WINTER?

Bears are famous for their long winter sleep, but do they hibernate? They certainly don't behave the same way as smaller hibernators.

How do animals hibernate?

When chipmunks or other small mammals hibernate, they lower their body temperature to just above freezing. Once a week, they wake, raise their temperature, eat stored food, and pass waste.

Do bears really hibernate?

Bears are different—they only lower their temperature a little. This made scientists think bears weren't truly hibernating—until they looked at the bigger picture. Bears in their winter sleep can go for 100 days without eating, drinking, urinating, or pooping!

HOW DO ELEPHANTS STAY COOL?

It's hot all year round on the African savanna, so these lumbering giants flap their huge ears to create a cooling draft!

African elephants also flap their ears to get rid of body heat, which blood vessels bring to the surface of the ears.

How much water does an elephant drink?

An elephant drinks up to 189 l (50 gallons) of water a day.

How else are big ears useful?

Elephants spread out their ears if they feel threatened. It makes them look even bigger than they already are!

ARE MAMMOTHS AND ELEPHANTS RELATED?

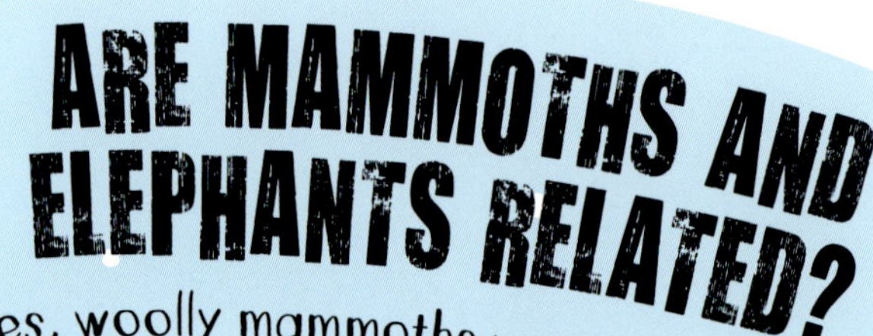

Yes, woolly mammoths were relatives of elephants that lived from 400,000 to 10,000 years ago, during the last Ice Age.

How did mammoths survive an Ice Age?

Woolly mammoths' ears were smaller than those of modern elephants, so they lost less body heat. Mammoths also had long, thick fur to keep out the cold. A hump behind their head stored fat, just like a camel's hump.

Were all mammoths huge?

Woolly mammoths stood 3.4 m (11 ft) tall at the shoulder. A dwarf species, just half this height, lived on Wrangel Island, off the coast of Siberia, until 4,000 years ago.

HOW MANY BUGS CAN A DRAGONFLY EAT?

An adult dragonfly eats hundreds of mosquitoes a day.

How big are dragonflies?

The largest living dragonfly is 10 cm (4 in) long with a wingspan of 19 cm (7.5 in).

Which fish is a shocker?

An electric eel can give off a charge of more than 500 volts.

How many eggs do toads lay?

Toads lay strings of eggs up to 6–20 m (20–66 ft) long.

A water flea is no bigger than a poppy seed.

Can mammals walk on water?

Yes, American water shrews are so light that they can walk on water!

How far can frogs leap?

Most frogs can jump a distance 30 times their own body length.

When were the first mayflies?

Mayflies appeared more than 350 million years ago—before the dinosaurs!

How can a spider breathe underwater?

A diving bell spider lives almost entirely under water in an air-filled web.

Do water scorpions sting?

Water scorpions don't sting with their long tails—they breathe through them!

ARE THERE CHIMNEYS UNDER THE SEA?

In parts of the seabed, "chimney pots" called black smokers gush out hot water that has been heated under Earth's crust.

How are the chimneys formed?

The hot water spurts out of a vent (hole) in the seabed. Grains in the water sink and pile up into chimneys around the vent. Bacteria feed on these minerals.

Does anything live on the smokers?

Giant red-and-white tubeworms are one of the creatures that feed on the bacteria around the black smokers. They can grow taller than basketball players—up to 2.4 m (8 ft).

How hot are the smokers?

Water gushing from a hot smoker can be up to 400 °C (752 °F)— as hot as a pizza oven!

WHAT ARE CORAL REEFS MADE OF?

Corals are made of tiny creatures called polyps. A coral reef builds up from the rocky remains of the polyps' skeletons.

How is a reef formed?

1. Polyps live in groups in warm, tropical seas.
2. When polyps die, their chalky skeletons are left behind.
3. Layers of skeletons build the reef up higher.

Living corals come in all kinds of shapes— some even look like brains!

Which is the world's largest reef?

The 2,300-km (1,430-mile) Great Barrier Reef contains more than 600 types of coral.

HOW BIG ARE EAGLES' NESTS?

The largest bald eagle nest, or eyrie, was 2.9 m (9.5 ft) wide and 6 m (19.7 ft) deep.

How can you keep a nest warm?

The Australian malleefowl's nest is a heap of rotting compost and sand. It keeps the eggs warm.

Where do coots nest?

Coots build nests on floating platforms.

Coot

Do birds live in cliffs?

Burrowing parrots nest in cliff holes. Some colonies contain up to 70,000 birds.

Which bird borrows nests?

The cuckoo lays its eggs in another bird's nest.

Cuckoo

European bee eater

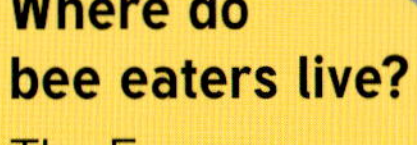

Where do bee eaters live?

The European bee eater nests in a burrow dug out of a riverbank.

Are nests reused?

Gyrfalcons reuse their cliff-ledge nests. One is 2,500 years old.

Gryfalcon

Which bird lives under a leaf?

The hooded oriole often builds its nest on the underside of a palm leaf.

Hooded oriole

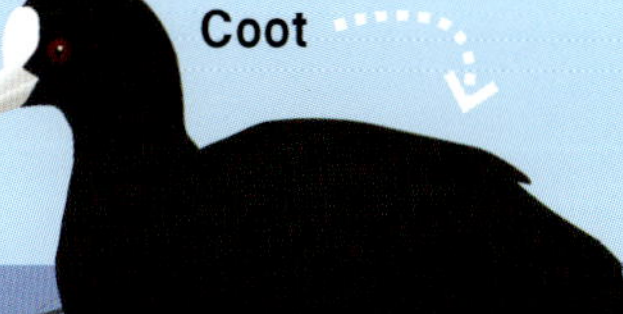

Which bird sews its nest together?

The tiny tailorbird stitches leaves with plant parts to make its nest.

Which nests are served as a meal?

The Chinese serve up swiftlets' nests, which are made of spit, in bird's nest soup.

WHICH ANTS STITCH THEIR NESTS?

Weaver ants make a home of leaves. They stitch them together with sticky thread.

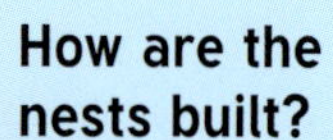

How are the nests built?

The adult ants collect the leaves. They link legs to form a chain and hold the leaves in position. Adults can't make thread, but larvae can—they are pressed over the joins like glue sticks!

How many ants live in the nests?

One colony can contain around half a million weaver ants.

Where are weaver ants found?

Weaver ants live in the tropics of Asia and Australia.

How strong is a weaver ant?

One weaver ant can hold up to 100 times its own weight.

WHICH INSECTS MAKE PAPER NESTS?

Paper wasps make amazing nests that look like works of art!

What are the nests like inside?

Paper wasps build their nest with flower-like layers. It has lots of compartments for their eggs and young, or larvae.

How are the nests made?

Paper wasps gather plant stems and tear strips of wood from trees or fences. They chew the plant material with spit to make a kind of paper.

How many types of paper wasp are there?

There are about 200 species of paper wasp.

How large are wasp nests?

The biggest-ever wasps' nest was 6.7 m (22 ft) long and housed more than 100,000 wasps.

WHOSE NEST IS WALNUT SIZED?

The world's smallest nest belongs to the tiny bee hummingbird. The nest is just 2.5 cm (1 in) wide!

Who builds the nest?

Hummingbird nests are made by the females, not the males. A bee hummingbird uses cobwebs, bark, and lichen for hers. Then she lays two tiny eggs, each no bigger than a pea!

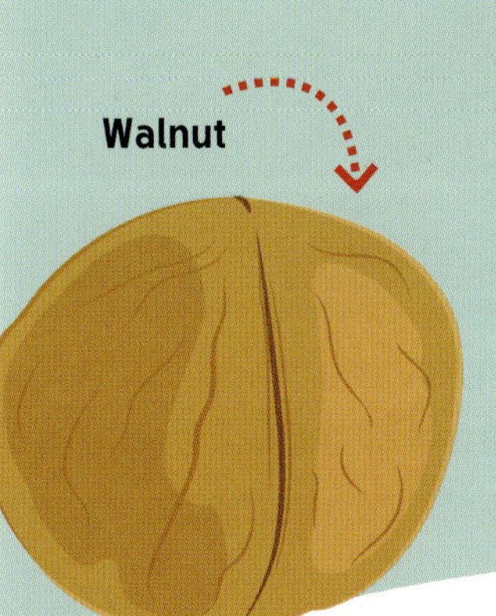

Are there any large hummingbirds?

The giant hummingbird is about ten times bigger than a bee hummingbird. Her nest measures about 20 cm (8 in) across. She weaves it from grass, moss, and spider webs, then lines it with soft animal hair and feather down.

Do turtles need helmets?

No, most turtles can tuck their heads into their shells for safety.

When did turtles first appear?

The first turtles lived alongside dinosaurs, around 215 million years ago.

WHERE DO TURTLES LIVE?

Turtles carry their home on their back in the form of a tough shell. It shelters them from the weather and protects them from danger.

What is the shell made of?

The turtle's shell is made of bone. The horned plates, or scutes, on top are made of keratin, the same material as your fingernails.

The flat underside of a turtle's shell is called the plastron.

Which turtle is the largest?

The leatherback sea turtle is the largest turtle in the world.

WHICH BIRD IS THE FASTEST?

The peregrine falcon's average diving speed is 322 kph (200 mph)—but it can plummet as fast as 389 kph (242 mph)!

Is there a faster falcon?

The gyrfalcon can outfly a peregrine falcon, although it cannot dive as fast. A peregrine's maximum flying speed is 110 kph (68 mph), while the gyrfalcon can fly at up to 145 kph (90 mph)—the same speed as a fastball in baseball!

Peregrine falcon

How fast do eagles dive?

A golden eagle's average dive speed is 241 kph (150 mph).

What about flying speed?

Homing pigeons reach speeds of 177 kph (110 mph). Swifts fly at 112 kph (69 mph).

Homing pigeon

WHICH ANIMAL IS FASTEST ON FOOT?

The cheetah is the fastest land animal. Its top sprinting speed is more than 100 kph (68 mph).

What makes a cheetah so fast?

- ✓ Long, thin legs
- ✓ Powerful muscles
- ✓ Long tail for balance
- ✓ Huge heart
- ✓ Stretchy spine

What do cheetahs hunt?

Cheetahs have to be swift to chase their fast prey! Speedy antelopes are on the menu, including springbok, gazelles, and impalas.

Cheetah

What makes cheetah feet special?

The cheetah's paws are different from those of other cats. The hard pads and non-retractable claws give extra grip at high speeds.

How wide is a cheetah stride?

A cheetah can cover 6.7 m (22 ft) in a single stride!

WHAT'S THE DIFFERENCE BETWEEN TOADS AND FROGS?

One of the ways to tell a toad from a frog is to look at how the animal moves.

Do toads and frogs move in different ways?

A toad's back legs are shorter than its head and body. It usually crawls along the ground, but it sometimes takes small hops. A frog has very long back legs with powerful muscles. It leaps high and long.

Do both have webbed feet?

Frogs spend most of their lives in or near water. Many species have webbed back feet to help them swim. Most toads don't have webbed feet.

WHAT WERE THE FIRST FLYERS?

The first flying insects appeared 400 million years ago (mya), about 80 million years after the first land insects.

Can all insects fly?

No, most ants, for example, can't fly.

When did flying insects first appear?

Wasps, bees, butterflies, beetles, and flies all evolved in the Cretaceous period (145–66 mya). They appeared at the same time as the first flowering plants.

What was the biggest dragonfly?

The prehistoric dragonfly Meganeura's wings were more than 75 cm (29.5 in) across. It lived around 300 mya and fed on other insects, which it caught on the wing.

CAN FISH WALK ON LAND?

Mudskippers live in muddy mangrove swamps and other shoreline habitats. Between the tides, when they are left out of the water, they "walk" around on their fins!

How does a mudskipper breathe?

A mudskipper can breathe through its skin if it's wet, just like a frog.

Mudskippers

Do other fish survive out of water?

The mangrove rivulus can spend more than two months out of the water. It hides inside a fallen log. Like the mudskipper, it breathes through its skin!

The walking catfish of Southeast Asia can wiggle to a new pool or swamp if it has to.

CAN SNAKES SWIM IN THE SEA?

All snakes can swim, but sea snakes actually live in the sea. They're usually found in tropical waters, around coral reefs.

How do snakes swim?

Snakes swim the same way that they travel across land. They move their bodies in an s-shape from side to side.

Are sea snakes dangerous?

Yes. There are around 50 sea snake species. They all inject their prey with paralyzing venom. The black-banded sea krait's venom is ten times stronger than a cobra's.

Black-banded sea krait

How strong is their venom?

Just three drops of venom from a beaked sea snake is enough to kill eight people.

WHICH ANIMAL IS TOP OF THE HOPPERS?

Boing! Boing! Boing! All four kangaroo species share one energetic feature—their main way of moving around is hopping!

Are kangaroos common?

Yes. There are more kangaroos than humans in Australia.

How do roos hop?

Kangaroos always move their back legs together when they hop, but they move them separately when they swim.

Which kangaroos can jump the farthest?

The red kangaroo is the largest, but it doesn't jump farthest or highest. That prize goes to the eastern grey kangaroo, which can cover 7.6 m (25 ft) in a single bound, and reach a height of 1.8 m (6 ft).

What do you call a group of kangaroos?

Kangaroos hang out in groups called "mobs." A mob can contain up to 100 kangaroos.

HOW HIGH CAN FLEAS LEAP?

Relative to their size, fleas are the best jumpers in the animal kingdom, leaping 100 times their height!

What do fleas feed on?

Fleas are parasites. Each kind specializes in a particular host, such as a cat, dog, or human. It sucks the host's blood for a while, then moves off. It might have to make as many as 10,000 jumps before it lands on a new host.

How fast can a flea jump?

A flea jumps with the same amount of acceleration as a space rocket.

How much blood can a flea drink?

A flea can drink 15 times its own body weight in blood!

CAN ELEPHANTS, HIPPOS, AND RHINOS JUMP?

No, these animals don't have flexible enough ankles to propel their bulk into the air.

Elephant

Rhino

Hippo

What is unusual about the way elephants run?

Unlike most animals, elephants don't take all four feet off the ground when they run.

Who charges fastest?

Rhinos can run faster than elephants. They charge at 55 kph (34 mph). Elephants can only reach 40 kph (25 mph), and hippos only 30 kph (16 mph).

CAN EMUS WALK BACKWARD?

Emus are big, flightless birds, related to ostriches and cassowaries. Unlike ostriches, emus are unable to walk backward.

Emu

What makes an emu unique?

The emu is the only bird that has calf muscles.

Is walking backward a useful ability?

Walking backward is a useful skill, especially when an animal is being threatened. No one knows why emus cannot do it. After all, they can't even fly from danger!

Which other animals from Australia only move forward?

Emus live in Australia, and so does another animal that can only go in one direction. All the traits that help the kangaroo take great forward bounds—its large feet, muscular legs, and big tail— also prevent it from going in reverse.

HOW SLOW ARE SLOW LORISES?

The slow loris is a big-eyed primate that can spend hours not moving if threatened. It will remain motionless until the danger has passed.

Slow loris

Where do lorises live?

Slow lorises live in Southeast Asia and are nocturnal hunters. They can cover a distance of 8 km (5 miles) in a night. They have an unusual way of moving, kind of like a snake.

How light are lorises?

Slow lorises are rare and small. The largest species weighs less than two bags of sugar. The smallest weighs just 400 g (14 oz).

Are lorises dangerous?

Yes, the slow loris has a venomous bite!

WHAT IS THE WORLD'S SLOWEST REPTILE?

The giant Galapagos tortoise ambles along at just 0.26 kph (0.16 mph).

What is the slowest bird?

The woodcock is the slowest bird. It flies along at just 8 kph (5 mph).

How long does a Galapagos tortoise live for?

The Galapagos tortoise takes its time living, too—it doesn't reach maturity until age 25 and it can live to more than 150! Like all reptiles, the Galapagos tortoise cannot make its own body heat. It spends a couple of hours basking at the start of the day to warm up.

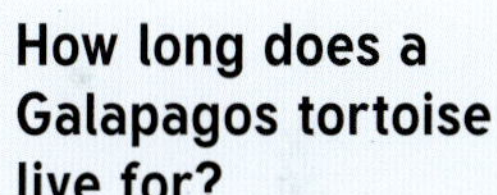

Galapagos tortoise

How slow is a snail?

A garden snail can only travel 1 m (3.3 ft) per hour.

COULD DINOSAURS OUTRUN TODAY'S REPTILES?

The fastest reptile around today is the bearded dragon, which dashes along at 40 kph (25 mph). The green iguana is next at 35 kph (22 mph).

How fast was a Velociraptor?

This deadly predator could sprint at 60 kph (40 mph). *Velociraptor* means "speedy thief."

Could an iguana outrun a T.rex?

If they'd lived in dinosaur times, the bearded dragon and green iguana could have escaped a *T. rex*, which only moved at 19 kph (12 mph). But they couldn't have outrun *Ornithomimus* or *Gallimimus*. Those "ostrich mimics" bounded along at 72 kph (45 mph)!

WHICH INSECT IS THE FASTEST?

The Australian tiger beetle runs at 6.8 kph (4.2 mph). That may not sound fast, but it's the equivalent of 171 body lengths a second.

How does this compare with animals and humans?

A cheetah travels 16 body lengths per second. Usain Bolt, the world's fastest man, covers six body lengths per second when he's sprinting.

Which is the fastest bug?

The record for the fastest land animal relative to body length is held by another creepy-crawly. A mite from southern California has been recorded at a speed of 322 body lengths per second. Mites aren't insects. They are arachnids, part of the same group as spiders.

WHICH BIRD IS THE SPRINTING CHAMP?

The ostrich is the fastest bird on land. It runs at 70 kph (43 mph)—as fast as a greyhound!

Who are the closest relatives of ostriches?

Rheas, emus, and cassowaries. The top speed for rheas is 64 kph (40 mph); for emus and cassowaries, it's 50 kph (31 mph).

Where do ostriches live?

Ostriches live in the African savanna and desert. They share their habitat with lions, leopards, and cheetahs ... which is a good reason to run fast!

What makes an ostrich fast?

- ✓ Two toes per foot
- ✓ Large, hooflike toenails
- ✓ Powerful, long legs
- ✓ Killer kick

CAN GECKOS WALK UPSIDE DOWN?

Yes. Geckos' feet can stick to any surface, no matter how smooth or slippery.

What's the tiniest gecko?

The smallest gecko is less than 2 cm (0.8 in) long.

How do they do it?

Millions of microscopic hairs on its toe pads give the gecko its amazing grip. Each hair has hundreds of even more microscopic bristles. These hairs and bristles stick to surfaces like Velcro®.

How big do geckos get?

The largest gecko was 60 cm (23.5 in) long.

Why are they called geckos?

The name gecko is meant to sound like the chirruping call it makes.

How many species of gecko are there?

There are nearly 1,000 species of gecko.

ARE WORMS HAIRY?

A worm's body appears to have smooth segments. Seen through a microscope, however, it has groups of rough bristles on its underside.

Who likes to chew on worms?

Birds, toads, moles, beetles, snakes, and foxes all like to make a meal out of a worm.

How long was the longest worm?

The world's biggest worm was found in South Africa. It was 6.7 m (22 ft) long!

How do worms move?

The earthworm moves its bristles in and out to get a grip on the ground. It moves its segments forward or backward by stretching and contracting its muscles.

How do slugs slide?

Land slugs and snails move along on one large, muscular foot. This glides on a glittering trail of mucus produced by a gland just under the mouth. Slugs and snails belong to a special group of mollusks called gastropods, meaning "stomach foot."

What is snail mucus?

It's more than 95 percent water, but snail slime has some amazing properties. It sticks the snail to surfaces and stops its body from drying out.

WHY ARE SLUGS AND SNAILS SLIMY?

Is it easy making slime?

A snail uses up nearly a third of its energy producing slime.

Do humans have a use for snail slime?

Snail slime is an ingredient in some face creams!

HOW FAST DO BEE WINGS FLAP?

A bumblebee beats its wings 200 times per second to stay airborne.

Bumblebee

Peacock butterfly

Can cockroaches take off?

Adult cockroaches have wings, but they rarely use them. They prefer to scuttle!

What makes flies so aerobatic?

A fly can move its two sets of wings independently.

House fly

Can butterflies fly if they're cold?

A butterfly's temperature must be around 29.5 °C (85 °F) for it to fly.

Can all moths fly?

The female winter moth's wings are too tiny for flight. Only the males can fly.

How fast are flies?

A blowfly travels at 8.6 kph (5.3 mph). Horseflies are much faster, at 40 kph (25 mph).

Blowfly

Are lice swift?

A headlouse can move 9.5 cm (3.75 in) per minute—the equivalent of the height of a giraffe in an hour!

Woodlouse

How many legs does a woodlouse have?

A woodlouse has seven pairs of jointed legs. It's a crustacean, related to crabs and shrimps.

The hummingbird hawkmoth beats its wings 85 times per second—about 1.7 times faster than a hummingbird.

Is a silverfish a fish?

No. The silverfish is a wingless insect. As it wiggles along, it looks like a fish.

Silverfish

WHICH BIRD FLIES BETWEEN THE POLES?

The Arctic tern flies at least 71,000 km (44,000 miles) a year, from the Arctic to the Antarctic and back again.

Can insects cross oceans?

Yes. Desert locusts have migrated 4,500 km (2,795 miles) across the Atlantic.

Which bird flies the farthest?

Bar-tailed godwits make the longest single flight of any bird, from Alaska to New Zealand.

Where is the world's largest mammal migration?

Each year, 1.7 million wildebeest trek through Tanzania and Kenya. Their journey is called the Great Serengeti Migration. Nearly half a million antelopes and 300,000 zebras also take part.

How far do tuna swim?

Bluefin tuna swim epic distances of up to 10,500 km (6,500 miles) to their spawning grounds.

Spiny lobsters march along the seabed to deeper waters each winter—a distance of up to 50 km (30 miles) each way.

Do elephant seals migrate?

Elephant seals make two 21,000- km (13,050- mile) migrations every year.

Do any creatures migrate up and down in the sea?

Zooplankton migrate up and down. Swarms swim a vertical distance of 3,000 ft (915 m) every day.

Where can you see millions of crabs?

In the wet season, 120 million red crabs migrate from the inland forests on Christmas Island. They travel to the coast to lay their eggs.

Do bats take a break?

Each year, ten million fruit bats travel up to 2,000 km (1,250 miles) to different feeding grounds in Zambia.

DO LEATHERBACKS GO LONG DISTANCE?

One tagged turtle swam an extraordinary 20,558 km (12,774 miles) across the Pacific in 647 days.

Where do leatherbacks live?

Leatherbacks live in the Pacific and Atlantic oceans. Pacific ones spend summer stuffing themselves with jellyfish off the coast of California. Their nesting beaches are in Southeast Asia. Atlantic leatherbacks feed off the east coast of Canada and nest in the Caribbean.

How big are leatherback turtles?

Leatherbacks are the largest sea turtles. They can weigh up to 900 kg (2,000 lb)—that's as much as a cow—and they are longer than a kingsize bed.

DO EELS HAVE FAR TO GO?

The European eel makes a mammoth migration of up to 6,000 km (2,730 miles), and it even slithers across land!

Are eels born long, thin, and wriggly?

Eels begin life as plankton-like larvae in the open ocean, leave it as pencil-sized young elvers, then return years later as adults. In between, they live in rivers and streams. Their leathery, slime-coated skin allows them to cross land to find new habitats.

Why do eels travel so far?

Male eels spend up to 12 years in fresh water, and females up to 20. Then they make the long journey back to the ocean to breed. Their dark bodies turn silver for better camouflage in the open ocean.

DO SNAKES HAVE EYELIDS?

No, these reptiles wear "glasses" instead!

Do snakes replace their eye scales?

A snake loses its eye scales when it sheds its skin—there are new ones waiting underneath. Just before shedding, the eye scale turns cloudy.

How do snakes stop their eyes drying out?

Rather than having movable eyelids, a snake has one clear scale over each eye. The scale protects the eye from damage and drying out.

What other animal lacks eyelids?

Fish don't have eyelids, either.

Can snakes blink?

No. They sleep with their eyes open, too.

CAN GIANT CLAMS SWIM AROUND?

Some animals, including giant clams, reach a stage in their lives when they won't travel anymore.

How are clams born?

Giant clams have a very complicated life cycle. They hatch into tiny swimming trochophores and then become plankton—part of the ocean "soup" of larvae, other small creatures, and plants.

Where can you find clams?

Giant clams pass through several more life stages before they reach their adult form. Then they settle on the reef or seabed and never move again.

Do other sea creatures stay put?

Adult barnacles never move, either!

CAN SNAKES SEE HEAT?

The infrared (IR) spectrum is invisible to humans, but not to snakes.

How do snakes detect infrared?

Rattlesnakes, boas, pit vipers, and other snakes can "see" body heat coming off their victims. They don't detect IR with their eyes, but with sensors between their eyes and nostrils. This super sense allows them to strike with deadly accuracy.

Rattlesnake

Can snakes sense footprints?

Snakes even detect body heat lingering in animals' tracks. It's as if they have built-in night-vision goggles or a thermal camera!

Which other animals see infrared?

- ✓ Mosquito
- ✓ Piranha
- ✓ Goldfish

CAN ANIMALS SEE IN ULTRAVIOLET?

Ultraviolet (UV) is another kind of light that humans can't see, but some animals can.

Butterfly

What appears different in ultraviolet?

Many flowers need insects to visit them to pick up pollen and carry it to other flowers. Some have UV markings that are only visible to bees and butterflies. These markings guide the insects in like landing-strip lights!

Human view (no UV sensitivity)

Bee view (UV sensitivity)

Do insects have hidden markings?

Some birds and butterflies have patterns on their feathers or wing scales that are only visible in UV. We can't see them, but their mates can!

Bee

ARE MOLES BLIND?

Moles have teeny-tiny eyes that can tell the difference between light and dark, but not much else.

What about a mole's other senses?
A mole spends its life underground. It uses its outsize front feet to scoop out tunnels. Other senses—touch, smell, and hearing—make up for the mole's lack of sight.

Are mole-rats related to moles?
Naked mole-rats aren't moles or rats. They're close relatives of guinea pigs. Like moles, they are nearly blind. They live in underground colonies of 20 to 300 animals.

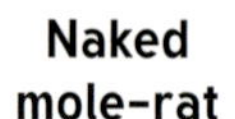

DO EARTHWORMS HAVE EARS OR EYES?

No, a worm's most important sense is touch.

How do worms feel?
An earthworm's body is covered in sense organs and nerve endings. The sense organs can "smell" and taste", while the nerve endings are for touch. They detect different textures in the worm's surroundings and pick up vibrations.

How many different kinds of worm are there?
There are about 6,000 different species of earthworm.

Can a worm sense light?
An earthworm may not have eyes, but it can still sense light. It needs to avoid sunlight, which can dry out its skin.

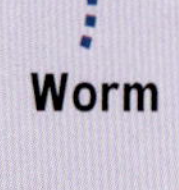

HOW SENSITIVE IS A LUNA MOTH?

A male luna moth's feathery feelers can sniff out a female 11 km (6.5 miles) away.

Caterpillar

Which moth tricks bats?

Tiger moths can not only hear bats' sonar—they can jam it! The moths confuse the bats by creating fake echoes.

Do caterpillars have eyes?

Unlike adult butterflies, caterpillars can hardly see. Their simple eyes sense only light and dark.

How many eyes does a praying mantis have?

The praying mantis's main sense is sight. It has two large eyes and three simple eyes located between them.

Praying mantis

Are wasps super-sniffers?

Wasps have an amazing sense of smell. They can even be trained to sniff out explosives and drugs.

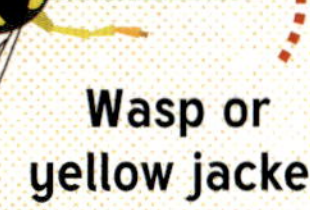

Wasp or yellow jacket

Which insect has the most taste?

Ants have about 400 smell and taste receptors—more than any other insect. Fruit flies have 61.

Where are a cricket's ears?

A cricket's ears are tiny—and they're not where you'd expect. They are just under the insect's knees.

Cricket

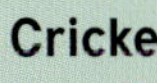

Cricket

The cockchafer beetle can fan out the end of its feelers. This helps it to sense sounds and smells, and find food.

Cockchafer beetle

Which beetles like fire?

Fire beetles flock to forest fires to lay their eggs in burned wood. Infrared sensors under the beetles' legs show them the way.

Can flies taste with their feet?

A fly has sensory hairs all over its feet. It can taste something by walking on it!

Fly

CAN OWLS SEE 360 DEGREES?

No. Owls do have enormous, forward-facing eyes but they sit in bony eye sockets so cannot move.

How far can an owl turn its head?

An owl cannot move or swivel its eyes, but it still has good all-around vision. That's because it can turn its head up to 270 degrees left or right, and almost upside down!

What use is binocular vision?

Forward-facing eyes give an owl good binocular vision (seeing an object with both eyes at the same time). That means it can see in three dimensions (height, width, and depth) and can also judge distance.

WHO HAS THE BIGGEST EYES?

The colossal squid has the largest eyes. It's also the world's biggest invertebrate!

How big are its eyes?

Each of the colossal squid's eyes is 30 cm (12 in) across—the size of a dinner plate! But very few of these creatures have ever been seen. Some individuals might have even bigger peepers!

Does anything hunt these sea giants?

Sperm whales hunt colossal and giant squid.

Where do colossal squid live?

The colossal squid grows to 15 m (50 ft) or more. It hunts in deep waters around Antarctica. Its slightly smaller cousin, the giant squid, has eyes that are 25.4 cm (10 in)—about the size of a basketball.

WHICH MAMMAL HAS THE BIGGEST PEEPERS?

Tarsiers have the largest eyes ... relative to their size, at least!

What do they measure?
Each eye is only about 0.6 in (16 mm) across, but a tarsier's whole body is only about the same size as a squirrel!

How heavy are its eyes?
Each of the tarsier's eyes weighs more than its brain!

Why does it need such large eyes?
Big eyes let in maximum light, and the tarsier certainly needs it. This little primate is a night hunter in the rain forests of Southeast Asia. It catches insects, small birds, bats, lizards, and snakes.

DO ALL SPIDERS HAVE EIGHT EYES?

About 99 percent of spider species have four pairs of eyes.

Do spiders see through all eight eyes?
Usually positioned on the sides of the head, the spider's smaller eyes are just simple sensors. They detect light, dark, and movement. So not all spiders' eyes have very good vision.

Which spiders have the best sight?
Daytime hunters, such as jumping spiders, have better eyesight than ones that are active at night. Their larger, forward-facing eyes pick out details and even different shades!

What about the 1 percent?
Some spiders have no eyes. Others have as many as six pairs!

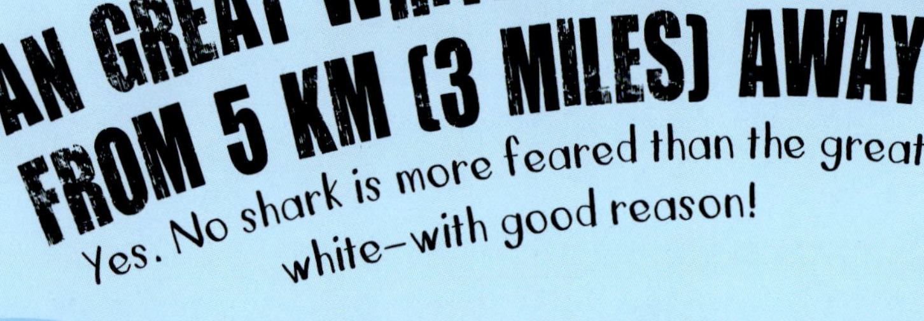

CAN GREAT WHITES SMELL BLOOD FROM 5 KM (3 MILES) AWAY?

Yes. No shark is more feared than the great white—with good reason!

Great white shark

Sharks use their sense of smell to find a mate and to navigate, too.

How do sharks smell?
Seawater washes smells into the great white's nostrils. If the shark smells prey—especially an animal that is already injured and weak—it heads toward it.

Great white shark

How much brain-power does it need?
Two-thirds of the great white's brain is used for processing smell.

How sensitive is its sense of smell?
A great white can detect one drop of blood in one million drops of water.

Does a shark have any other special senses?
As well as being able to see, hear, feel, smell, and taste, sharks detect electrical signals.

Can transparent fish be seen?
Cuttlefish and octopuses can "see" transparent sea creatures by how the light bounces off their bodies.

Narwhal

Is a narwhal's tusk sensitive?
Nerves in a narwhal's tusk can sense changes in water temperature.

When a horse curls its upper lip, it's processing smells. It can tell if there's danger—or a suitable mate—nearby.

Catfish

What are a catfish's whiskers used for?
The catfish's "whiskers" help it smell and taste.

Can a platypus sense electricity?
Yes, a duck-billed platypus senses electricity given off by its prey. It has special receptors on its bill.

A four-eyed fish has two eyes, but four pupils. Each eye can see above the water and below.

Duck-billed platypus

CAN ANIMALS PREDICT WEATHER?

Some animals can tell when a storm's on the way—especially prey animals, such as wild sheep and goats.

Why are jerboa ears so large?

A jerboa's huge ears give it keen hearing. They also release body heat and keep it cool.

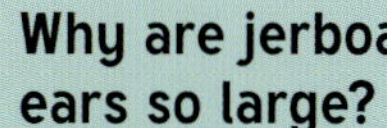

Do lizards have a third eye?

Most lizards have a "third eye" on the top of their head that is sensitive to light.

Can dogs help doctors?

Dogs seem to detect cancer and other medical conditions. They can smell chemical changes in their owners.

How do bats see in the dark?

Bats use a form of sonar. They squeak then see how long the echoes take to come back. It tells them what's near.

DO WOLVES REALLY HOWL AT THE MOON?

No. Wolves howl to communicate with each other.

How far can a wolf's howl travel?

A wolf's howl can be heard up to 16 km (10 miles) away.

Do all wolves sound the same?

Different wolf species have their own "accents," or dialects.

Do wolves howl together?

Packs of wolves sometimes howl together as a chorus.

How do wolves howl?

Wolves are most active at night, so that's when they need to communicate. They point their face up when they howl to make the sound carry farther. They look as if they are howling at the sky.

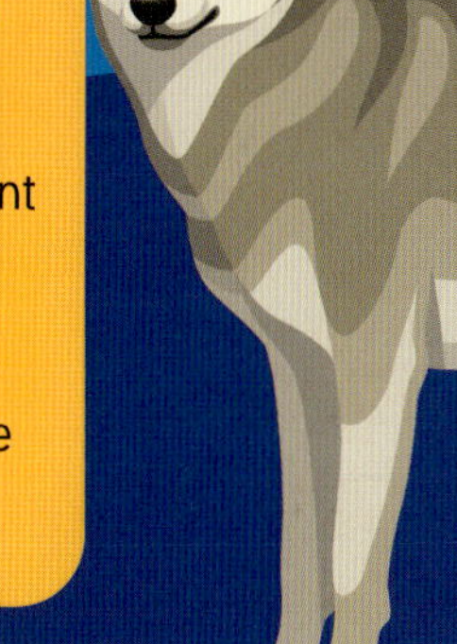

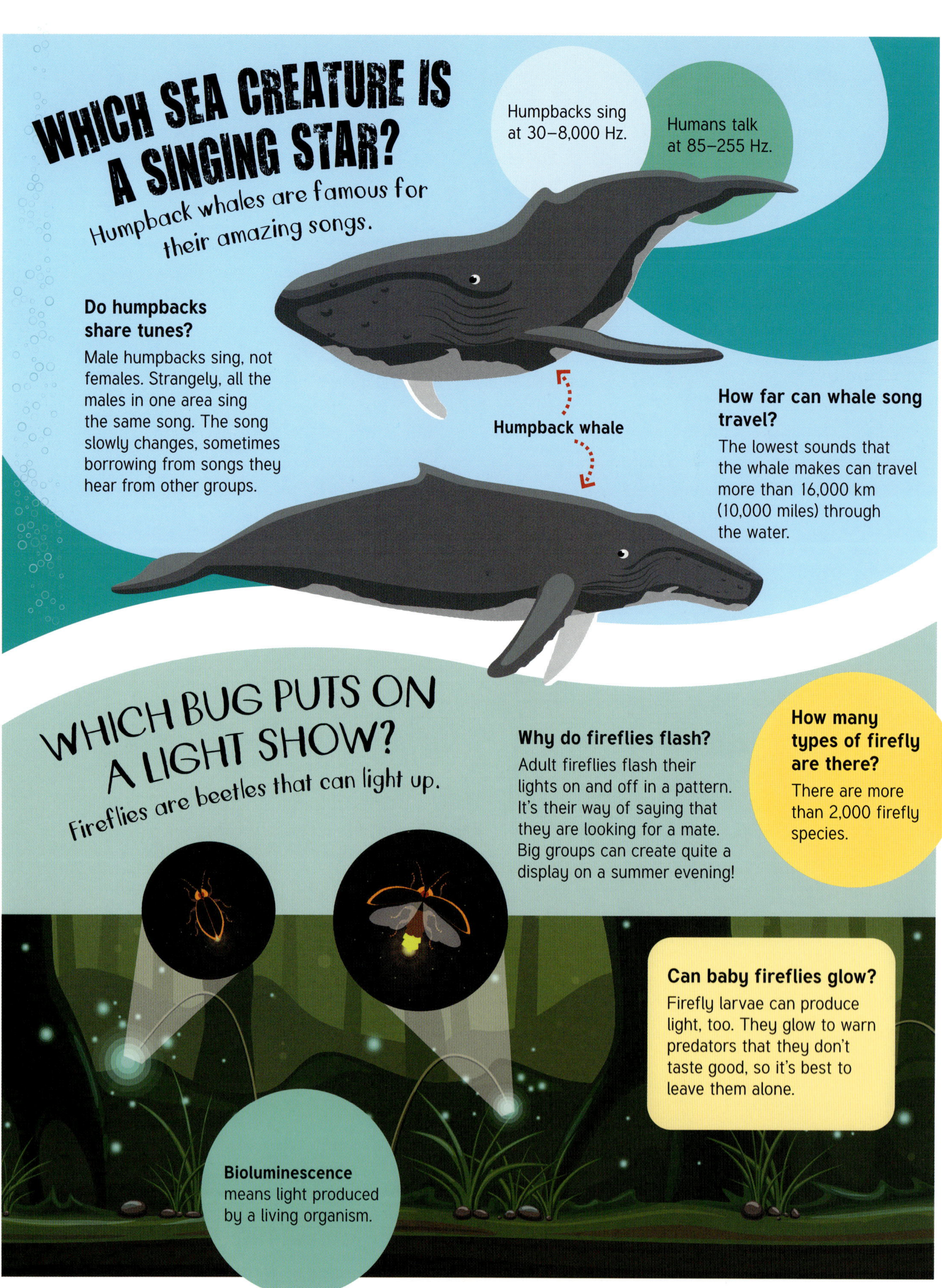

WHICH SEA CREATURE IS A SINGING STAR?

Humpback whales are famous for their amazing songs.

Humpbacks sing at 30–8,000 Hz.

Humans talk at 85–255 Hz.

Do humpbacks share tunes?

Male humpbacks sing, not females. Strangely, all the males in one area sing the same song. The song slowly changes, sometimes borrowing from songs they hear from other groups.

Humpback whale

How far can whale song travel?

The lowest sounds that the whale makes can travel more than 16,000 km (10,000 miles) through the water.

WHICH BUG PUTS ON A LIGHT SHOW?

Fireflies are beetles that can light up.

Why do fireflies flash?

Adult fireflies flash their lights on and off in a pattern. It's their way of saying that they are looking for a mate. Big groups can create quite a display on a summer evening!

How many types of firefly are there?

There are more than 2,000 firefly species.

Can baby fireflies glow?

Firefly larvae can produce light, too. They glow to warn predators that they don't taste good, so it's best to leave them alone.

Bioluminescence means light produced by a living organism.

WHICH SNAKE IS A MASTER MIMIC?

The harmless milk snake is disguised to look like the deadly coral snake. Both are red, black, and yellow.

Which animals sprays blood?

The horned lizard has a repulsive way to discourage predators. It fires blood at them from its eyes!

Horned lizard

The rough-skinned newt has an orange belly—a warning for predators that it contains poisons.

Why should you avoid a sea slug?

The sea slug has stinging cells to protect itself. The bright skin warns would-be hunters.

Sea slug

Which fish has a "mane?"

The lionfish is named for its frilly "mane." It helps the fish look bigger than it really is.

Lionfish

Why do some animals have large spots?

Huge spots can be mistaken for eyes that belong to a much larger creature.

Pink butterfly fish

Which bird has a smelly secret?

The hoatzin's other name is the "stink bird." It deters predators by smelling like cow dung.

Hoatzin

Which bug uses chemical warfare?

The bombardier beetle sprays explosive chemicals at any attacker. BOOM!

Which small bird does impressions?

A tiny bird called the brown thornbill can mimic the call of a hawk. It does this to scare predators away from its nest.

Why should you give a skunk plenty of space?

A skunk scares off bears or other predators by squirting a foul, stinky liquid from its anus!

Skunk

WHICH BUG PRETENDS TO BE A WASP?

Hoverflies have yellow-and-black markings, just like wasps or hornets.

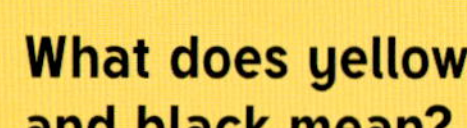

How does this disguise help the hoverfly?

Even though they aren't dangerous, being disguised to look like wasps means that hoverflies are not eaten by birds or other predators. These animals move along in case they get stung!

What does yellow and black mean?

Wasps and hornets wear yellow and black as a warning sign. It tells other insects that they carry a painful sting, so it is best to steer clear.

WHY DO FRILLED LIZARDS PUFF OUT THEIR NECKS?

It's a trick to make the lizard look bigger!

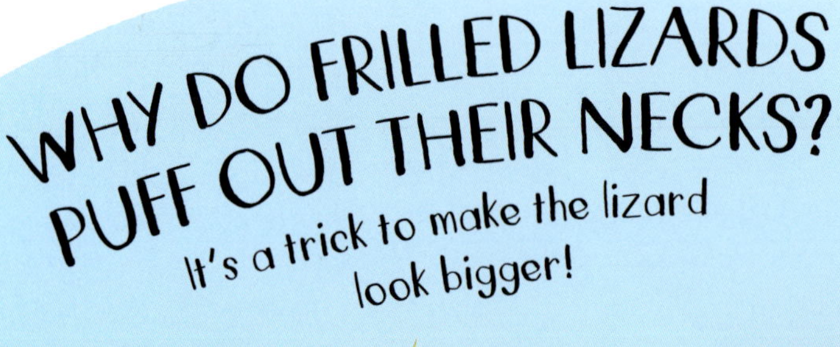

When does the lizard display its frill?

The frilled lizard has a pleated flap of skin around its neck. If it feels threatened, it unfurls its neck frill and hisses. If this display doesn't terrify the attacker, the little lizard races up the nearest tree.

Where do frilled lizards live?

Frilled lizards live mostly in the trees, except when they're tempted down to catch smaller lizards, rodents, or other prey.

How big are frilled lizards?

Frilled lizards are up to 90 cm (3 ft) long.

Are the lizards born with a frill?

Frilled lizards hatch from their eggs as miniature adults, complete with a working frill!

WHY DO PUFFERFISH BLOW THEMSELVES UP?

These strange little fish blow themselves up when they feel threatened.

When do puffer fish inflate?

There are around 190 species of pufferfish. None are a typical fish shape—some even look like little cubes or pyramids. When threatened, they puff up to show off their prickly spines.

Why are pufferfish a risky meal?

Pufferfish contain deadly toxins. Strangely, their meat is a delicacy in some parts of the world. Trained chefs remove most of the toxins, leaving just enough to give the diner a tingly tongue!

DO MOSQUITOES HUM TO ATTRACT A MATE?

Yes. The buzz of a mosquito isn't just a warning that you are about to be bitten! The sound helps them to attract a mate.

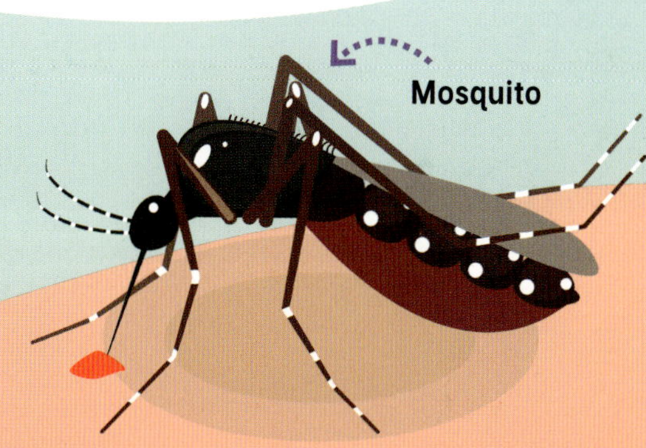

What makes the buzz?

The buzzy hum comes from the mosquito's moving wings, which beat up to 600 times per second. When a male and female meet, their wings rise and fall in time and produce the same hum! How romantic!

Do all mosquitoes bite?

Male mosquitoes feed on nectar, but females need to suck blood to nourish their eggs. Their bites can be deadly.

What diseases can mosquitoes carry?

- ✓ Malaria
- ✓ Yellow fever
- ✓ Dengue fever
- ✓ Encephalitis

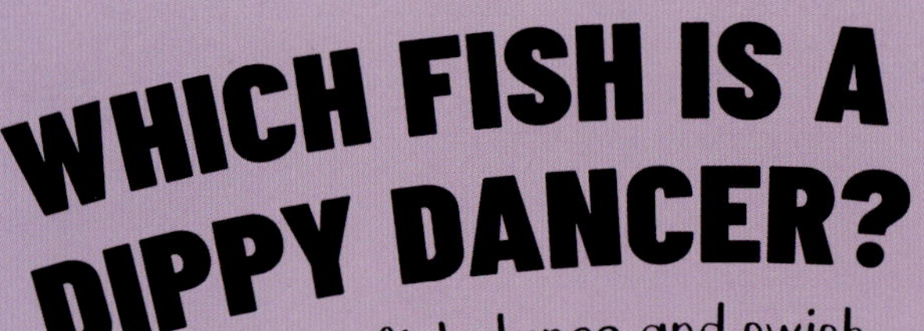

WHICH FISH IS A DIPPY DANCER?

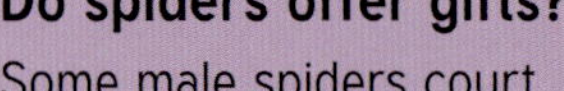

Male guppy fish dance and swish their tails to attract a mate.

Male peacocks start to grow their fancy tail feathers at the age of two.

Peacock

Do spiders offer gifts?

Some male spiders court females with a silk-wrapped present of food.

How do cranes find partners?

Red-crowned crane couples perform complicated courtship dances.

The male peacock spider displays the flashy markings on its abdomen to a female—just like a feathered peacock shows off its blue-and-green tail!

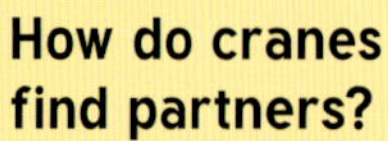

Red-crowned crane

How do stags dress to impress?

Stags roar to interest females. They may drag their antlers through a bush, too. If they snag some vegetation, it'll make them look bigger!

When are fine feathers not enough?

Bright feathers aren't enough for the male bird-of-paradise—it puts on an acrobatic display, too!

Bird-of-paradise

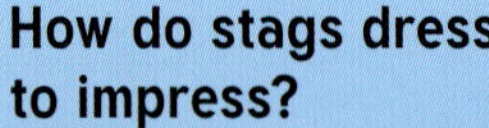

Stag

The male frigate bird has a huge, bright-red, inflatable throat sac. When it's puffed out, the females certainly notice him!

Which mammal has a nose for the ladies?

The male hooded seal has a pink "nose balloon." He attracts attention from females by inflating it.

Hooded seal

Why would you not want to be a female hippo?

Male hippos and porcupines court females by peeing on them.

WHICH BIRD BARKS LIKE A DOG?

The clue to the mockingbird's trick is in its name. It "mocks" another animal's call!

How many tunes can it sing?

A mockingbird can learn 150 songs or more.

How close are a mockingbird's copies?

The male mockingbird can copy other birds' songs. To human ears, his songs sound like exact copies, but female mockingbirds can tell the difference.

Mockingbird

How does this impress females?

Females choose the males that sing the most songs. Maybe it's a way of guaranteeing a mature mate—after all, it takes time to learn all those calls.

What do mockingbirds copy?

Mockingbirds mimic noises made by frogs, dogs, and car alarms!

WHICH PARROT MAKES A RACKET?

Kakapos are the noisiest parrots.

How far away can you hear a kakapo?

The male kakapo's low, booming call to attract a mate can travel as far as 5 km (3.1 miles). To amplify the sound and bounce it farther, the male digs out a little bowl-shaped stage and stands in the middle of it!

Why is the kakapo critically endangered?

The kakapo lives in New Zealand. It had no natural predators there, so it lost the ability to fly. Later, this made it easy prey for dogs and other transplanted animals. Today there are fewer than 160 kakapos left in the wild.

WHAT IS THE LOUDEST MONKEY?

This howler monkey's howl can be heard through thick forest from 5 km (3 miles) away!

Howler monkey

Why do they howl?

Howler monkeys are South America's biggest monkeys. They live in troops of up to 20. Each troop has its territory, and the males howl to defend it.

How loud are they?

Howler monkeys are especially noisy at the start and end of the day. Their calls can reach 128 decibels, making them the loudest land animal.

Howler monkey

How big is a howler monkey's tail?

A howler monkey's tail is about as long as its head and body together—up to 92 cm (36 in)!

DO WALRUSES WHISTLE?

Yes. They also bark, grunt, bellow, growl, rasp, and click!

Why do walruses have such a range of sounds?

For everyday communication, walruses bark—just like their close relatives, seals and sea lions. But at breeding time, bulls (males) show off many more calls. Most are produced by the vocal cords, but there are also spooky, bell-like sounds from inflatable air sacs in the throat.

How long are walrus tusks?

Male walruses communicate with their tusks. They show off their length—up to 90 cm (3 ft)—and bash rivals with them!

How heavy are walruses?

Walruses are HUGE! They can weigh up to 1.4 tonnes (1.5 tons)!

Walrus

ARE ORCAS SCARIER THAN SHARKS?

Orcas (also called killer whales) and sharks are the ocean's apex predators.

What makes orcas especially dangerous?

Apex predators are right at the top of the food chain, with no other animal hunting them. Sharks have a fierce reputation, but at least most species work alone—orcas hunt in groups like wolf packs.

Why do orcas come ashore?

Some clever killer whales deliberately "beach" themselves to catch seal pups. They know that the next wave will carry them back out to sea.

Are orcas smart?

An orca's brain weighs nearly 200 times more than a great white shark's.

WHAT ARE THE BIGGEST LAND PREDATORS?

Polar bears and Alaskan brown bears are huge hunters.

What do bears eat?

Bears will eat anything! Brown bears are famous for catching salmon in early summer. Polar bears hunt seals, birds, and fish. Both bears hunt mammals too, from rodents to reindeer.

Do bears eat greens?

Meat is only a small part of a brown bear's diet. Mostly it feeds on grass, fruit, insects, nuts, roots, and leaves. Polar bears sometimes eat kelp or berries.

WHY ARE BLACK MAMBAS DOUBLY DEADLY?

These venomous snakes are also very fast movers!

How deadly is a mamba bite?

A bite from a black mamba can kill a person in 20 minutes.

How fast are black mambas?

Over short distances, a black mamba can probably hit speeds of 20 kph (12.5 mph). Once it catches its prey, it delivers a paralyzing bite. Then it waits for the poison to take effect.

What do black mambas eat?

Black mambas hunt bats, chickens, bushbabies (a kind of primate), and other snakes. They live in grasslands and forests in sub-Saharan Africa.

WHICH SNAKE HAS THE LONGEST FANGS?

Gaboon vipers, and they also pump out more venom than other snakes.

How long are the fangs?

A Gaboon viper's fangs are 5 cm (2 in) long. Once they pierce a victim's flesh, they can inject a couple of teaspoonfuls of venom. The snake is an ambush killer. It lies hidden on the forest floor and then strikes a passing bird or mammal.

How heavy are Gaboon vipers?

Gaboon vipers can grow to 1.8 m (6 ft) long and weigh more than 20 kg (45 lb). They are Africa's heaviest venomous snake.

DO JELLYFISH LASSO?

Long tentacles help the jellyfish to catch a meal.

How do jellyfish stun their prey?

Stinging cells along the jellyfish's trailing tentacles snag on plankton, crustaceans, and small fish. The stingers have barbs that inject poison and paralyze the prey.

Which sea creature steals stings?

Sea slugs prey on jellyfish and steal their stings. First, the slug slimes all over the jellyfish so it cannot fire defensive stinging cells. Then, when the slug eats the jellyfish, the stingers pass to pouches on its body. The slug can fire them out if it comes under attack!

DO DRAGONS EXIST?

The reptile with the deadliest bite is the Komodo dragon.

Are Komodo dragons cannibals?

Yes! Younger Komodos make up a tenth of an adult's diet!

Is the Komodo the world's largest lizard?

Yes, the Komodo dragon is about the same length as a tiger. It's named after one of the Indonesian islands where it lives.

What do the dragons prey on?

Mostly, the Komodo dragon eats carrion. But it also kills large prey, including water buffalo, deer, pigs, monkeys, and even humans. Its jaws aren't very powerful, but it has a venomous bite and sharp, knifelike teeth.

WHICH SPIDER HIDES INDOORS?

The trapdoor spider's burrow has a hinged trapdoor. The spider bursts out to catch insects, frogs, and mice.

The cunning cougar stalks through the undergrowth … and then pounces.

Cougar

The yellow-tailed scorpion strikes woodlice by the entrance to its lair.

Yellow-tailed scorpion

Common snapping turtle

Which turtle plays statues?

The common snapping turtle "hunts" by staying very still. If prey comes close, the turtle's head darts forward to snap it up.

Which fish is camouflaged like coral?

The scorpionfish has mottled skin to blend in with its coral habitat. It has toxic venom to paralyze prey.

The cookiecutter shark ambushes prey bigger than itself. It bites cookie-sized chunks from its victim's flesh.

Some mantis shrimps dart out at prey as fast as 2.3 m/s (7.5 ft/s).

Grouper

Which fish is a sucker for prey?

The grouper's big-lipped mouth sucks in passing prey.

Which lizard changes its shades?

The chameleon is an artful ambusher. Its skin can change to be brown, green, blue, orange, or more.

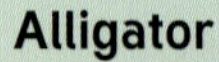

Alligator

Is that a log in the water?

An alligator looks like a floating log—until it rears from the water and attacks.

DO LEOPARDS KEEP SECRET FOOD SUPPLIES?

Like most big cats, the leopard hunts solo and hides its catch for later.

Leopard

Where is a leopard's pantry?

The leopard drags carcasses high into a tree to eat over a few days. This big cat eats prey of all sizes, from monkeys to baby giraffes. It is usually active at night and is a powerful swimmer, runner, and climber.

How strong is a leopard?

A male leopard can drag prey weighing 180 kg (400 lb) into a tree—that's three times its own weight!

Why are leopards spotted?

The leopard's rosette pattern helps it approach its prey without being noticed.

DO HYENAS EAT LEFTOVERS?

Hyenas are famous for scavenging food from lion kills

Can hyenas eat bones?

Striped and brown hyenas feed mostly on carrion, but 95 percent of the spotted hyena's diet is meat that it has hunted and killed. Hyenas live and hunt or scavenge in packs. Thanks to their amazing, bone-crushing teeth, they eat every last bit of a carcass.

Spotted hyena

Striped hyena

Are hyenas at risk?

Striped and brown hyenas are both near threatened status.

What's so funny about hyenas?

Spotted hyenas are sometimes called laughing hyenas, because they make a creepy laughing noise. They are the most common large carnivores in Africa.

CAN AFRICAN WILD DOGS OUT-HUNT LIONS?

Fewer than a third of lion attacks end in a kill, but African wild dogs have an 80 percent success rate!

African wild dog

Why are wild dogs so successful?

African wild dogs work together to surround a herd of prey animals and separate off a weak individual. They also take turns when it comes to the chase, so no dog becomes too tired.

How many animals are in a pack?

An African wild dog pack contains 20 animals or more. The top breeding pair are the leaders. However, they don't get first pickings at a feast—youngsters do!

ARE CATERPILLARS EATING MACHINES?

Yes! They have huge appetites.

How fast do caterpillars grow?

Caterpillars are the larvae (grubs) of butterflies and moths. They have strong jaws for munching. They eat constantly, sometimes doubling in size in just a few days.

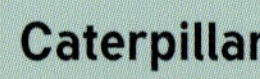

Caterpillar

What do caterpillars eat?

Most caterpillars feed on plants. Others have more expensive tastes. Clothes moth caterpillars chomp through silks, wools, and other costly fabrics, ruining people's garments.

Do caterpillars get overweight?

Caterpillars eat so much that their skin gets too tight. They have to shed their skin several times!

How do secretary birds tackle snakes?

Most birds of prey hunt from the air, but the secretary bird spends most of its time on land. It is large and powerful, with muscular legs. It kills or paralyzes snakes and lizards by jumping on their backs over and over again.

WHICH BIRD STOMPS ON SNAKES?

The secretary bird–it jumps on snakes to kill them.

Secretary bird

How does the bird swallow a snake?

The secretary bird tears up prey into bitesize chunks with its sharp talons. When it attacks smaller prey, such as insects, mice, and hares, it uses its bill, not its feet.

WHICH BIRD DRILLS FOR DINNER?

A woodpecker uses its sharp beak to peck at poles and trees.

The woodpecker's toes provide a strong grip.

Red-headed woodpecker

How does a woodpecker reach food?

Holding out its stiff tail feathers for support, the woodpecker drills the wood to reach beetle grubs, other insects, and sap with its extra-long tongue.

Pileated woodpecker

It has a long tongue for licking up sugary sap.

What gives a woodpecker such great grip?

Most woodpeckers have two toes that face forward and two that face back. It gives them a stronger grip than most birds, which usually have three forward-facing toes and one facing back.

How fast does a woodpecker hammer?

A woodpecker can peck up to 20 times per second!

CAN MONKEYS USE TOOLS?

Some macaques use stone tools to crack open nuts and shellfish.

Where do they find food?

The crab-eating macaque lives in lots of different habitats in Southeast Asia. In coastal areas, the monkey dives for crabs, sea snails, and oysters. It smashes the shells with a stone.

What else do they eat?

Macaques are omnivores—they eat plant food, meat, and fish. Fruit makes up a big part of their diet. They are also a pest, stealing sugarcane, sweet potatoes, and other crops from farms.

DO FISH PROVIDE SERVICES?

Cleaner wrasses are small, busy reef fish that clean larger fish and turtles.

Where do fish go for a clean up?

Animals of the coral reef visit "cleaning stations" to be cleaned by the cleaner wrasses. Sometimes they even line up, waiting their turn. The little fish nibble off dead scales, slime, or parasites and their visitors leave looking clean and tidy!

What do wrasse get in return?

The wrasse get a free meal (of delicious dead scales and parasites). Cleaner shrimp offer a similar service, even clambering around inside a predator's mouth.

WHO'S NOT AFRAID OF SCORPIONS?

Meerkats! They are not bothered by the sting in a scorpion's tail.

How do they dodge the sting?

The stinger at the end of a scorpion's tail pumps deadly venom into an attacker—but a meerkat won't give it the chance. It quickly bites off the scorpion's stinger then eats the rest of the creature at its leisure.

What are meerkats?

Meerkats belong to the mongoose family. Insects make up most of their diet, but they also eat fruit, eggs, and various animals, including snakes and scorpions.

Can meerkats be hurt by the sting?

A meerkat isn't immune to venom—if a deadly scorpion managed to deliver a sting, the meerkat wouldn't survive.

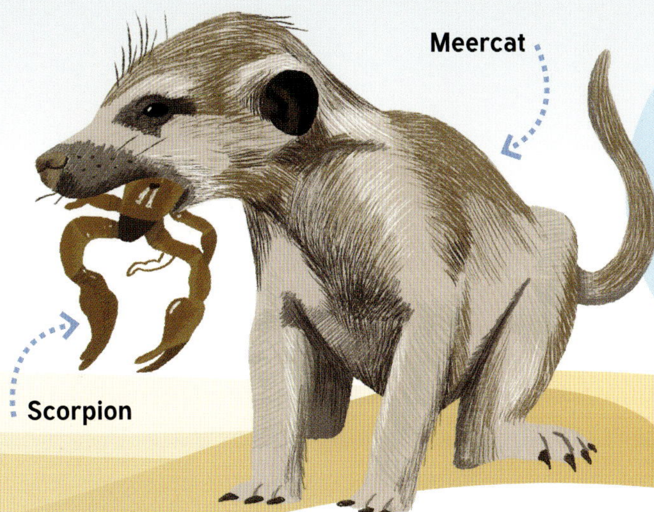

ARE FLAMINGOS BORN PINK?

Chicks are born with dull downy feathers, not flamboyant pink ones!

How do flamingoes turn pink?

A flamingo's diet slowly turns its feathers orange or pink over time. It eats algae and shrimps, which contain natural dyes called carotenoids.

What else eats carotenoids?

Carotenoids are what give wild salmon healthy-looking, deep-pink flesh. Koi carp breeders deliberately feed carotenoids to their fish. It helps deepen their brilliant red and orange scales.

Do other foods contain carotenoids?

Humans eat carotenoids, too—they are found in carrots, sweet potatoes, tomatoes, and greens.

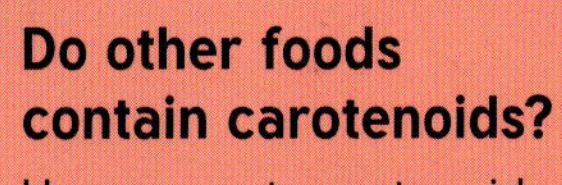

WHICH RHINO IS THE FUSSIEST EATER?

The black rhino's diet includes more than 200 kinds of plant. White rhinos eat only grass.

Capybara

Which animal eats rocks?

Pangolins hunt at night for termites and ants. They swallow rocks to help digest them.

Capybaras live near rivers and lakes in South America. They gnaw reeds, grains, melons, and squash.

Which creature gobbles gravel?

The duck-billed platypus doesn't have a stomach with acids to digest food. It breaks down food in its mouth by mashing it with gravel.

Which fish shoots their prey?

Archerfish target insects on overhanging branches. They fire drops of water at them.

Archerfish

Duck-billed platypus

Do all horseflies suck blood?

Female horseflies have piercing mouthparts to suck blood from livestock and people. Males feed only on pollen and nectar.

Which mammal is a snake scrapper?

The Indian grey mongoose fights cobras and eats them. It's resistant to small amounts of venom.

Redknee tarantula

Which bug bothers tarantulas?

The small-headed fly lays her eggs on a tarantula. When they hatch, the larvae eat the spider from the inside out.

Tiger

What do tigers eat?

Tigers mostly prey on deer, wild pigs, and buffalo. They will even eat baby elephants.

Which animal takes a long meal break?

The giant isopod, a deep sea crustacean, can last for five years without eating.

ARE PIRANHAS BLOODTHIRSTY MANEATERS?

Not all are dangerous. There is even a vegetarian species of piranha!

What about the meat-eaters?

Piranhas have a bad reputation. In times when food is scarce, one drop of blood in the water will attract schools of piranhas. The fish can strip a carcass clean with their razor-sharp teeth.

Which fish has the strongest bite?

The black piranha has the strongest bite force of any bony fish.

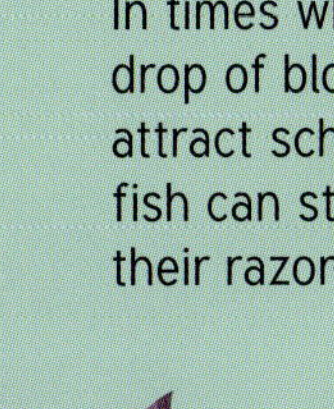

Do piranhas attack humans?

Most of the time, piranhas eat plants, insects, snails, and smaller fish. They eat more seeds than meat! They don't pass up the opportunity if an easy meal falls into the water, but they rarely attack humans.

WHAT IS THE WORLD'S MOST DANGEROUS ANIMAL?

Diseases transmitted by mosquitoes kill millions of people every year.

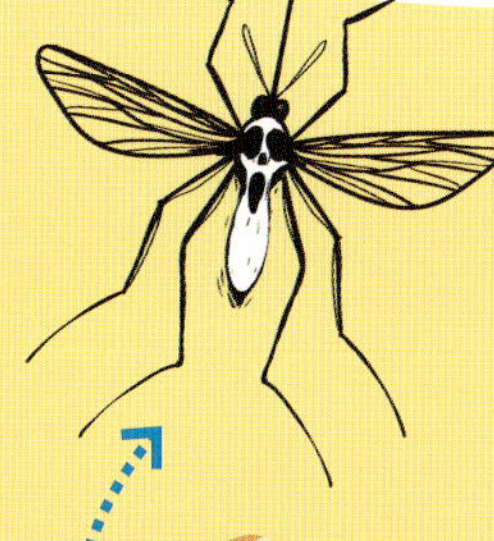

Are all mosquitoes bad?

There are more than 3,500 types of mosquito, but only a couple of species are primarily responsible for spreading disease.

How dangerous is malaria?

One million people die of malaria each year.

How are mosquitoes harmful?

Mosquitoes can carry parasites, viruses, and bacteria. When a mosquito feeds, these microbes can enter a person's bloodstream and cause disease, including malaria.

WHICH BIRD EATS EARWAX?

The oxpecker eats earwax—it has very strange eating habits!

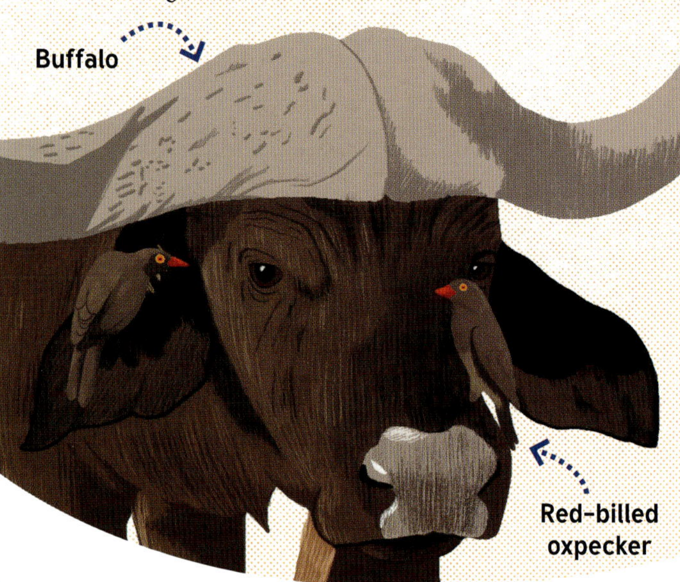

What does an oxpecker peck?

The oxpecker lives in the African savanna. It picks ticks, lice, and maggots off large grazing animals. Its hosts include giraffes, antelope, buffalo, and rhinos.

There are two oxpecker species—red-billed and yellow-billed.

Do they eat hair too?

No. Oxpeckers pick hair off their hosts to line their nest holes.

So, are oxpeckers helpful?

Picking off parasites is good, but the oxpecker is a kind of parasite itself! It feeds on the host's earwax and skin. It even pecks open scabs to drink its host's blood.

DO SOME ANIMALS EAT THEIR OWN POOP?

Yes! Rabbits, hares, and some rodents eat their own poop.

Why would an animal do this?

These animals eat hard-to-digest stems and grasses. By gobbling freshly-made poop, they give their body a second chance to extract the nutrients from a meal.

Poop-eaters
- ✓ Rabbits
- ✓ Guinea pigs
- ✓ Hares
- ✓ Chinchillsa
- ✓ Gophers
- ✓ Lemmings
- ✓ Voles
- ✓ Kangaroo rats

Why do beetles gather poop?

Some insects have a taste for poop. Flies and dung beetles lay their eggs in it, so that their babies hatch in a ready supply of food. Yummy!

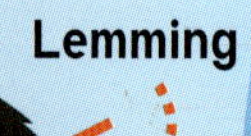

WHICH ANIMALS ARE HARDEST TO SEE?

The pygmy seahorse is almost impossible to spot. It's tiny, and looks like its pink coral habitat.

Leafy sea dragon

Fish or seaweed?
The leafy sea dragon is another well-disguised seahorse. Its fins sway like fronds of seaweed.

Why turn white?
Many polar animals are white. The Arctic owl's pale feathers hide it from foxes and wolves in the snow.

Arctic owl

Walking sticks or stick insects are green or brown. Their thin bodies mimic branches.

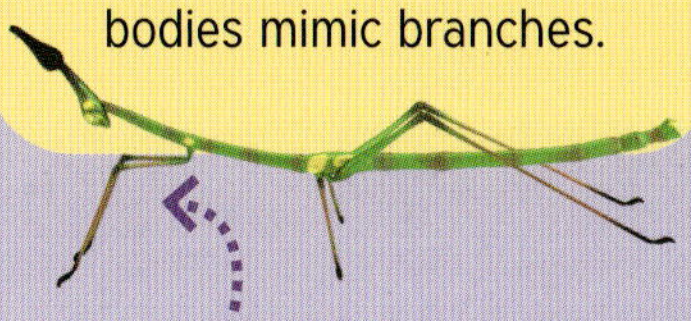

Stick insect

Leaf costumes are a great disguise. The leaf-tailed gecko is a master.

Why would a duck be dull?
Many female ducks have dull feathers. It stops predators spying them on their nests.

A mossy frog's bumpy green skin looks just like moss.

Pheasant

Why are things looking up for bitterns?
The bittern is a wetland bird. When it stands still, beak pointing skyward, it could be mistaken for a reed!

Flounder

Flounders are well camouflaged against a sandy or pebbly seabed.

Are pheasants too bright to hide?
A pheasant's feathers blend in with the ground, soil, and leaves.

The leaf frog is almost invisible in leaf litter. It resembles an old leaf.

Leaf frog

HOW DO ANTEATERS CATCH ANTS?

Anteaters lap up ants with a super-long and super-stretchy tongue.

The anteater's appearance is strange enough before it opens its mouth, thanks to its long, narrow snout. However, its weirdest feature is its flexible tongue, designed for slurping up ants.

How long is the tongue?

A giant anteater is 2.1 m (7 ft) long—and its narrow, spine-covered tongue is a whopping 0.6 m (2 ft)! It flicks it in and out of an anthill up to 160 times per minute. The anteater works quickly to avoid being bitten by the ants.

Do anteaters bite or chew ants?

No, anteaters don't have any teeth.

Anteater

DO ANIMALS WASH THEIR FOOD?

Yes, Japanese macaques use sea or river water to rinse food.

How did it begin?

It all started when a female monkey had the bright idea of washing the soil off her food. Before long, the rest of the troop was copying her!

How do macaques cope with winter?

The Japanese macaque is nicknamed the "snow monkey" because its home, in northern Japan, is snow-covered for much of the year. That doesn't bother the monkeys, though—they keep warm by bathing in hot springs.

Japanese macaque

Do any other monkeys live in any cold places?

Snow monkeys live in a colder climate than any other primate—except humans!

ARE PANDAS PICKY EATERS?

Bears might like a varied diet, but not giant pandas!

Are pandas in danger?

There are only 1,864 pandas left in the wild. Their bamboo forest habitat is being cut down.

What do pandas eat?

Around 99 percent of the panda's diet is bamboo, but it isn't very nourishing. A panda must eat up to 38 kg (84 lb) of bamboo every day.

Panda

Do pandas have thumbs?

Pandas have evolved an extra sixth digit or "thumb." They use it to grasp bamboo stems.

American crocodile

Crocodiles appeared ten million years before the first dinosaurs.

CAN ANIMALS GO MONTHS WITHOUT EATING?

Crocodiles can last over a year without a meal.

Nile crocodile

How long can a crocodile go without food?

In the 240 million years that crocodiles have been on the planet, they've seen some tough times. They often go without food for a few months, but if necessary they can survive for over a year.

How do crocs save energy?

Crocodiles don't use much energy. They hardly move and they don't make their own body heat.

WHAT ARE THE STRANGEST ANIMAL DIETS?

Which bird makes others retch?

The skua is a seabird. It will attack a seagull till it throws up, then eat the gull's vomit.

Skua

What is marine snow?

The vampire squid feeds on so-called "marine snow"—all the flakes of dead stuff that float down toward the seabed.

Which creature enjoys a family meal?

A tiger salamander will eat its own brothers and sisters!

Tiger salamander

Do birds drink blood?

The vampire finch is named for its habit of sucking the blood of booby birds.

Why are sharks dangerous before birth?

Tiger shark pups eat their brothers and sisters while they are still in the womb.

Tiger shark

Which beetle buries bodies?

Carrion beetles bury corpses. Once underground, they create food for baby beetles.

Carrion beetle

What eats its meals twice?

Cows' food returns to their mouth from their stomach for a second chew.

Cockchafer beetle

Cockchafer beetles lay their eggs in soil. Their larvae feed on plant roots.

CAN BEETLES CHOMP THROUGH HOUSES?

Yes! Some beetles eat wood!

Which bugs eat wood?

Powderpost beetles, deathwatch beetles, house longhorns, and furniture beetles are just some of the culprits. Their larvae, known as woodworm, spend years eating through floorboards, joists, and furniture.

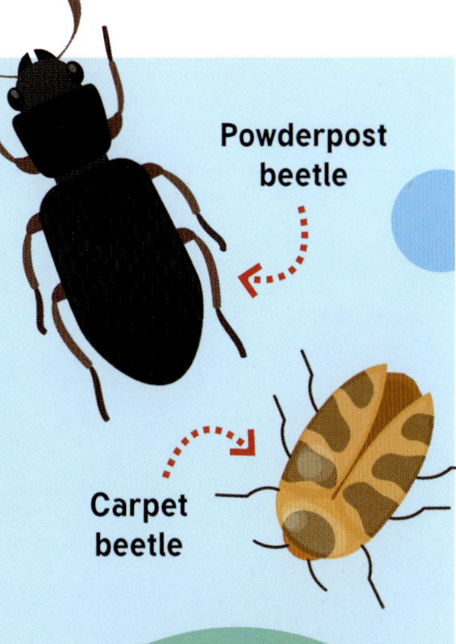

Which insects should you keep from your wardrobe?

Insect pests also eat clothes and carpets. Clothes moths and carpet beetles munch through silk, fur, cotton, and wool.

Which beetles are super spooky?

Deathwatch beetles tap on wood to attract a mate. People used to say the spooky sound meant death was on its way.

WHY ARE WEEVILS BORING?

Weevils have super-long snouts for "boring" into plants.

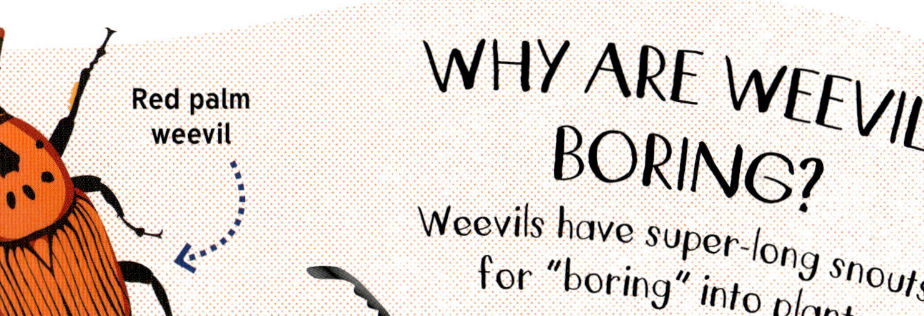

What do weevils munch on?

Weevils belong to the beetle family. Most feed on one kind of plant. The acorn weevil drills into acorns and the nut weevil into hazelnuts. Boll weevils eat cotton buds and flowers, grain weevils attack grain, and red palm weevils feed on coconut and date palms.

Can we eat weevils?

In parts of Southeast Asia, people eat red palm weevil grubs as a special treat.

Why does one weevil have a long nose?

Male giraffe weevils' snouts are especially long! They joust each other with them.

WHY ARE SOME CREATURES SLIMY?

Many creatures produce slime to defend themselves.

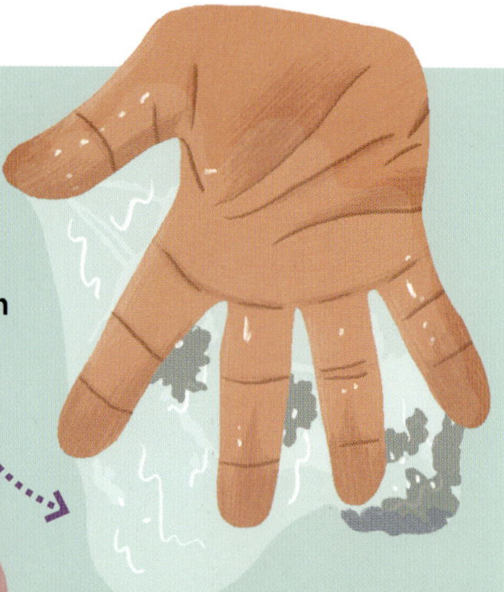

Why do predators avoid hagfish?

Hagfish have a disgusting habit. They ooze slime if they sense a fish about to attack. It's a great strategy because the slime clogs up the attacker's gills, so the predator soon backs off!

Hagfish slime

Hagfish

What sticky solution saves salamanders?

Amphibians are usually moist, but one salamander takes slime to a new level. When a slimy salamander feels threatened, it produces mucus. The gloop glues up the predator's paws.

WHY DO ANIMALS CURL UP?

Becoming a ball is a clever defensive strategy.

Even a lion can't get its teeth into a pangolin when it's in a ball.

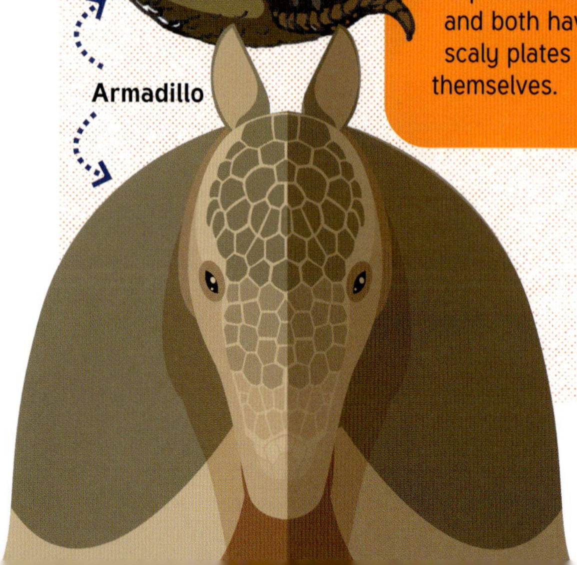

Who are the curled-up champs?

Armadillos and pangolins live on different continents, but they both curl up if a predator approaches, and both have protective, scaly plates to defend themselves.

Pangolin

Trilobite

Armadillo

Which ancient animal curled up for safety?

The first animals to defend themselves by rolling up were sea creatures called trilobites, millions of years ago. Their living relatives, woodlice, use the same technique.

WHY DO ANGLERFISH TEAM UP?

The anglerfish lives in the vast, deep ocean, where it's hard to find a mate.

Do male anglerfish merge with females?

Yes! Some anglerfish males are much smaller than the females. When the male finds a female, he clings on by his teeth. Over time, his body merges with hers. He loses his eyes and organs and becomes a parasite.

How many partners does a female take?

One female anglerfish can have more than six attached males. Her body supports and feeds them. In return, they fertilize her eggs.

How do anglerfish hunt?

A fishing rod "lure" sticks out over the female anglerfish's mouth. Its glowing tip brings prey close.

HOW HUGE ARE MALE ELEPHANT SEALS?

A southern elephant seal bull weighs up to 4 tonnes (4.5 tons).

Where do they live?

Southern elephant seals live around the Southern Ocean. Being large keeps them warm in cold seas and on harsh coasts.

What noise do elephant seals make?

The male elephant seal's trunklike nose makes his snorts, grunts, and bellows super-loud. The top, or dominant, bull in the colony mates with all the females.

Do elephant seals dive?

Yes, elephant seals can stay underwater for up to two hours.

DO RATTLESNAKES FIGHT?

Yes, rattlesnakes decide who mates with the females by having wrestling matches.

Stag beetle

Are stag beetle jaws just for show?
Male stag beetles do battle with their outside jaws, which look like stag's antlers.

Bighorn sheep

Which beasts butt heads?
Sheep and goats have headbutting contests to decide which male is the best.

Do female animals fight?
It's the female topi antelopes, not the males, who fight over a mate!

Pikas are mountain mammals, related to rabbits and hares. Rather than have physical fights, the males chase and taunt each other.

Male rhinoceros beetles use their rhino-like horn to fight other males.

Rhinoceros beetle

Moose

Fighting male moose lock their enormous antlers, which can be 1.8 m (6 ft) across.

Cardinal bird

How does a gorilla say he's boss?
Male gorillas usually decide who's dominant with hoots and chest-beating displays. If they do fight, it's to the death.

Why do hippos yawn?
A male hippo's toothy yawn is a sign of aggression. It means "back off, or prepare for a vicious fight!"

Do birds have fights?
From kingfishers to cardinals, many male birds have fierce fights over territory. They need it to attract a female.

Hippo

DO MALE SEA HORSES GIVE BIRTH?

Yes! The sea horse is the only animal where the male becomes pregnant!

Seahorse

How does this work?

A male sea horse has a pouch on his body. The female lays her eggs inside it and the male fertilizes them. The male carries the developing eggs, and gives them oxygen and food.

How many babies do sea horses have?

Small sea horse species have 50 to 150 babies at a time, but larger ones produce up to 2,000! Only about five in 1,000 of the babies, called fry, survive to have their own young. Sea horses are poor swimmers, but they can grip seagrass with their tails so the tide doesn't sweep them away.

DO PENGUINS MAKE GOOD DADS?

The female emperor penguin lays a single egg, which she gives to her mate to keep warm.

Where do the females go?

Each female heads off to sea for eight weeks to fill up on krill, fish, and squid. She returns just before her chick hatches. She provides its first meal by vomiting up partly-digested food. Yum!

How do males protect an egg?

The males huddle together for warmth, balancing their precious eggs on their feet. so they do not touch the ice.

How cold is the Antarctic?

Emperor penguins live in freezing-cold Antarctica, where temperatures drop to −60 ºC (−75 ºF).

Emperor penguin

Male emperor penguin

WHICH ANIMAL PRODUCES A BILLION EGGS?

Giant clams squirt out a billion eggs at a time.

How old do giant clams get?

A giant clam can live for a century or more.

Giant clam

About 65,000 animal species are hermaphrodites.

Why do they release so many?

Giant clams are huge—more than 135 cm (4.5 ft) long. An adult giant clam's body is cemented to a coral reef, so it cannot travel to find a mate. Instead, it releases clouds of eggs and sperm into the water. All the nearby clams do the same.

Are clams male or female?

Both! Animals that make both eggs and sperm are called hermaphrodites. Like the giant clam, most cross-fertilize—sperm from another animal fertilizes their eggs.

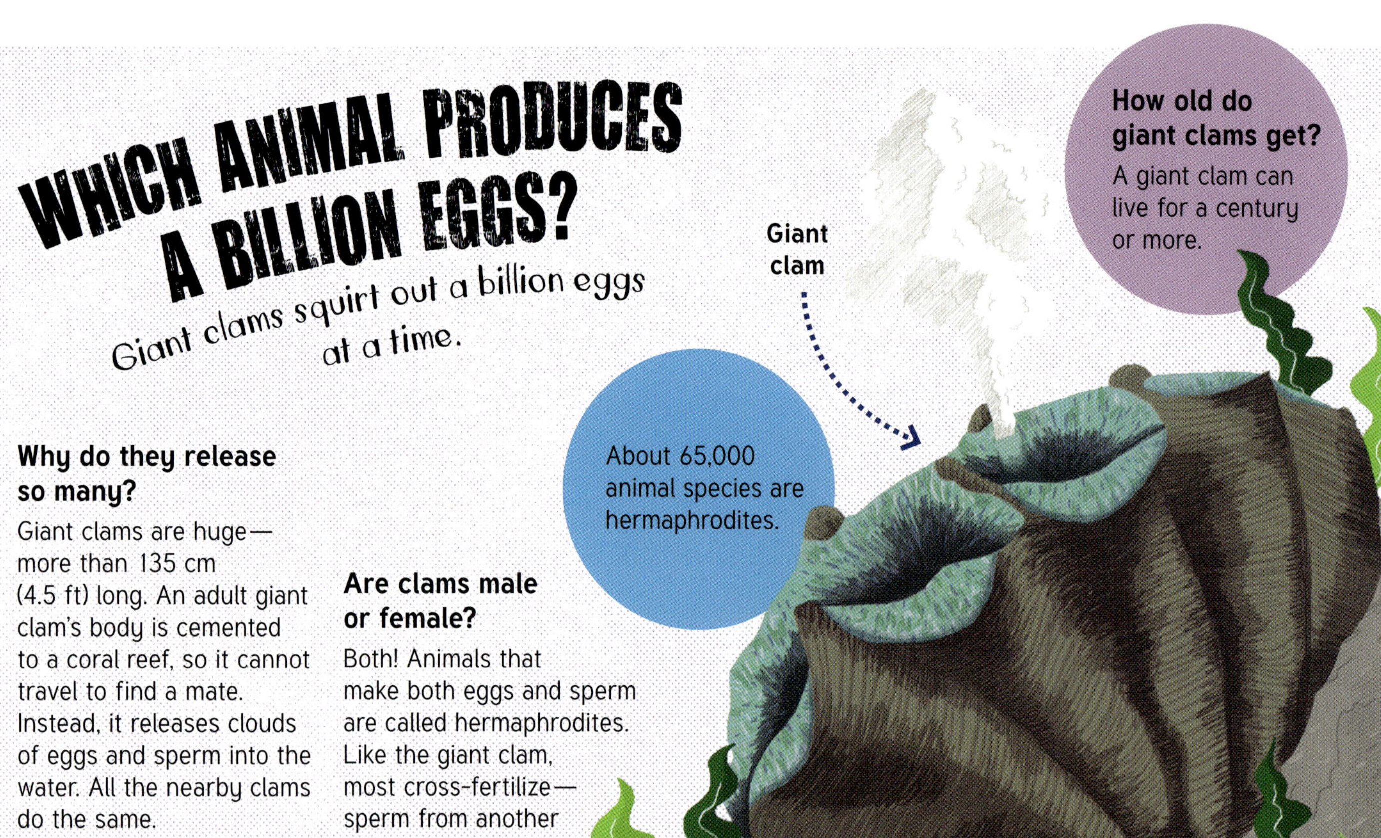

DO MAMMALS LAY EGGS?

Some do. The duck-billed platypus is one example.

What kind of animal is a platypus?

The platypus is a monotreme—a mammal that lays eggs instead of giving birth to live young. The female usually lays two eggs in her burrow. She keeps them warm until they hatch.

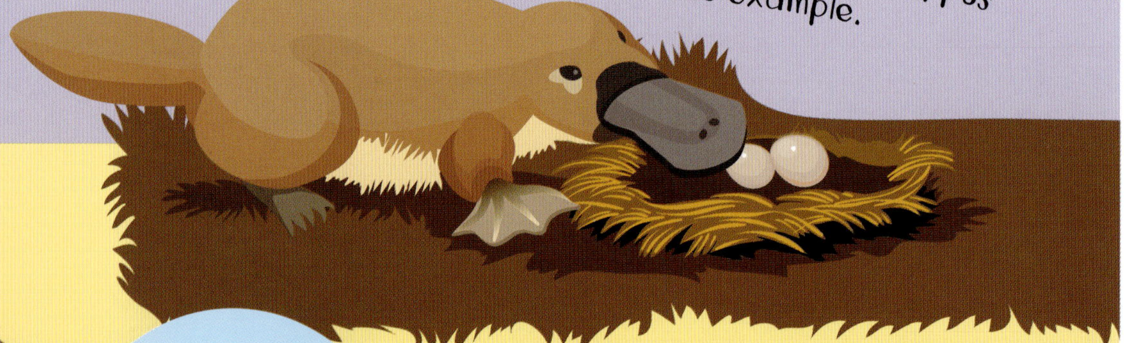

Duck-billed platypus

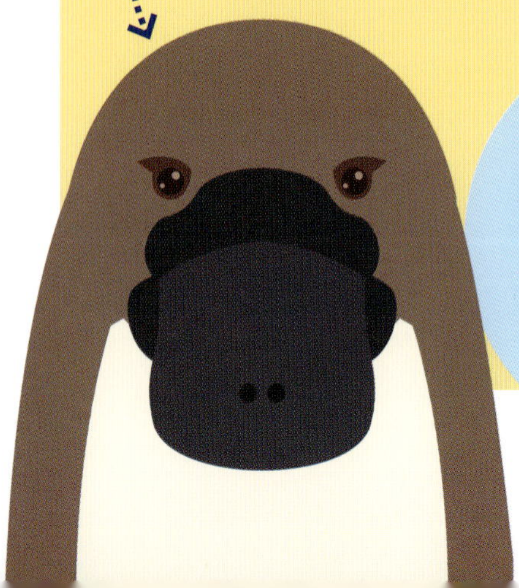

What other mammals lay eggs?

Echidnas are the only other egg-laying mammals.

What do platypus babies feed on?

Newly hatched platypus babies are bald and helpless. They drink milk, but their mother doesn't have nipples—the milk drips from her pores.

WHY ARE SNOWY OWL EGGS SO TOUGH?

Snowy owl eggs have thick shells to keep out UV rays from the Arctic sun.

Storm petrels' eggs can survive the Alaskan cold while their parents are away looking for food.

Storm petrels

Which animal lays strange eggs?

Horn sharks' eggs are in spiral-shaped egg cases. They screw them into gaps in the rocks.

What are mermaids' purses?

They are the washed-up empty egg cases of skates and dogfish.

Which bird lays the largest egg?

The ostrich lays 7–10 eggs at a time. It has the largest eggs—the record weight was 2.6 kg (5.7 lb).

Ostrich

Ostrich egg

Chicken egg

Skate egg case

Who carries eggs on their back?

A male midwife toad carries eggs on his back until they are just about to hatch.

Which bird keeps its eggs germ free?

Hoopoes cover their eggs with sticky, stinky brown slime. It contains bacteria that protect the eggs from infections.

Hoopoes

African foam-nest frogs lay eggs in meringue-like foam on branches over ponds. The tadpoles drop into the water when they're developed.

Foam-nest frog

Which mother gulps her eggs?

A cichlid mother stores developing eggs in her mouth for up to a month, until the fish are fully-formed fry.

The vervain hummingbird's egg is less than 1 cm (0.4 in) long.

Baby whale sharks develop in egg capsules inside the female's body. Each capsule is more than 60 cm (23.6 in) across.

HOW MANY BABIES DO SNAKES HAVE?

Not all snakes lay eggs—some give birth to live young, as many as 50.

Which snakes lay eggs and which have babies?

Snakes from cooler climates usually produce live babies. Baby rattlesnakes and vipers develop inside eggs in the mother's body, then hatch as live young. The eggs have yolks to nourish them.

Do boas have live young?

Boas, anacondas, and many sea snakes don't develop in eggs at all. As they develop, their mother feeds them through a placenta. Boas have from 15 to 50 snakelings!

More than two-thirds of snakes lay eggs.

WHY ARE BABY TURTLES IN SUCH A HURRY?

A newly hatched turtle must dash down the beach, to avoid predators.

Where are turtles born?

A female sea turtle lays her eggs on the beach where she was born. She comes ashore at night, scrapes a shallow nest, lays 80 to 120 eggs, covers them with sand, then returns to the sea.

What hunts baby turtles?

During their scramble to the sea, some turtles are eaten by crabs and birds, while others are baked alive in the sun.

Turtle eggs are soft and round, with a leathery "shell."

HOW MANY BABIES DOES A RABBIT HAVE?

A rabbit only lives for 12 years, but it produces about 1,000 kits (babies) in that time.

How soon can rabbits become mothers?

A female rabbit (doe) is fully grown at three months. After mating, she is pregnant for a month before she gives birth to her first litter of 5 to 12 kits.

What do kits feed on?

For the first three weeks, kits feed only on milk. Then they start to nibble grass, too, and their mother is free to feed her next litter.

Are female rabbits always pregnant?

A doe is pregnant non-stop through spring, summer, and autumn. She has a break over the winter.

DO ARMADILLOS HAVE IDENTICAL QUADRUPLETS

Yes! Armadillos are the only mammals—apart from humans—that consistently have identical babies.

Why so many quadruplets?

A nine-banded armadillo mother produces only one egg, but it splits into four as it develops. Each becomes a separate but identical baby. Each has exactly the same DNA.

Can armadillos jump?

A frightened nine-banded armadillo can leap 122 cm (4 ft) into the air!

Do armadillos care for their young?

Armadillo babies live with their mother in her burrow for at least a year. Over her lifetime, a female nine-banded armadillo has up to 56 young.

DO KOALA JOEYS EAT POOP?

Yes, it's called pap, and it helps a young koala move from milk to eucalyptus.

Eucalyptus contains toxins that are poisonous to most mammals, but not koalas.

Do koala joeys grow up in pouches?

Like a kangaroo, a newborn koala is tiny and undeveloped. It crawls into its mother's pouch, attaches to a teat, and continues to grow. At around six months old, it starts to feed on pap as well as milk.

What's the difference between poop and pap?

Ordinary koala poop is hard and dry but pap is runny. It passes important microbes from the mother to the joey. The youngster needs these to digest eucalyptus leaves.

ARE CROCODILES DEVOTED MOTHERS?

Many reptiles abandon their eggs, but not crocodiles!

How does temperature determine sex?

The crocodile lays her eggs in a mound of vegetation and pees on the mound to warm it! If the temperature in the nest is 31.7–34.7 °C (89–94 °F), the baby crocodiles will be male. Any cooler or hotter and the babies will be female.

How does a croc mum care for her young?

When they are ready to hatch, the crocodiles call from their eggs. Their mother comes and clears away the nest mound. She carries the hatchlings to the water in her tooth-lined mouth!

A crocodile lays 35–50 eggs.

ARE BABY PANDAS BLACK AND WHITE?

No, newborn panda cubs look pink!

How small are newborn pandas?

Apart from pouched mammals, such as koalas and kangaroos, panda mothers have the smallest mammal babies relative to their own size. A newborn panda weighs just 85–142 g (3–5 oz).

Do panda babies have fur?

Newborn pandas have a fine covering of white hair—so fine that the pink of their skin shows through. From about a week old, patches of black fur grow around the eyes, ears, and shoulders.

Are dalmatians born black and white?

Dalmatian dogs are prized for their black spots, but their puppies are usually born pure white!

DO SUNFISH BABIES WEAR STAR-SHAPED SUITS?

Yes. Adult sunfish look weird—but their offspring look weirder!

What do adults look like?

The ocean sunfish looks like a big blob! Weighing up to 1,000 kg (2,205 lb), it's the heaviest bony fish. It spends a lot of its time floating near the surface, sunbathing.

Which vertebrate lays the most eggs?

An ocean sunfish produces up to 300 million eggs per season—more than any vertebrate.

Sunfish fry

How do sunfish develop?

Surprisingly, the sunfish has tiny eggs that hatch into pinhead-sized larvae. The larvae have a transparent, star-shaped case. Fry—the next life stage—have spines, like puffer fish.

Sunfish fry

WHOSE MILK IS THE CREAMIEST?

A harp seal's milk is 12 times creamier than cow's milk.

How fast do seal pups grow?

Harp seal pups are born in the icy Arctic. Their mother nurses them with her energy-rich milk. The pups grow quickly. At three weeks they begin to use their fluffy white fur.

Do birds produce milk?

Pigeons, flamingos, and emperor penguins feed their chicks crop milk—fatty liquid produced in their crop (throat pouch).

ARE THERE CANNIBAL FROGS?

Strawberry poison-darts serve up eggs to their tadpoles.

How do frog parents stop the kids eating each other?

Poison-dart tadpoles are cannibals, so the parents raise them in separate pools!

How do you raise a poison-dart frog?

1. The father guards the eggs until they hatch.
2. The mother carries each tadpole to a different bromeliad plant.
3. For six weeks, the mother produces unfertilized eggs for the tadpoles.

How do tadpoles become poisonous?

The eggs give the tadpoles vital proteins and other nourishment. They also contain the dangerous poisons that protect poison-dart frogs from predators.

WHOSE EGG IS THE LARGEST FOR BODY SIZE?

A kiwi chick hatches from an egg that is 20 percent of its mother's own weight!

Kiwi

What is the record for kittens?

The largest litter of kittens was 19, born to a Burmese-Siamese crossbreed.

Burmese-Siamese kitten

Warthog

Baby warthogs are born with tusks!

How many cubs does a tiger have?

A mother tiger usually has three or four cubs. Sometimes she has a record litter of seven, but if this happens, four or five won't survive.

Are hippos born underwater?

Some baby hippos are. Their mother pushes them to the surface to take their first breath.

Hippo

How heavy is a whale calf?

A blue whale calf is the biggest baby—it weighs about 2.7 tonnes (3 tons) when it's born!

For how long do elephant calves drink milk?

Elephant calves drink their mother's milk for up to four years.

What is a puggle?

Echidna babies are called puggles. They have no hairs and no spines!

Elephant

DO SCORPION BABIES HITCH A RIDE?

A scorpion mother carries her young on her back. She defends them with the sting in her tail.

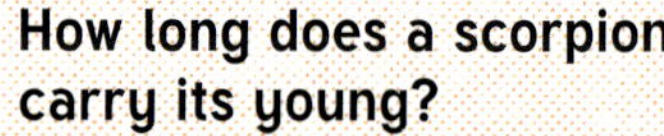

How many babies does a scorpion have?

A scorpion mother has up to 100 babies at once. They don't hatch from eggs like spiders—they are born alive, and crawl onto her back.

How long does a scorpion carry its young?

The mother carries the babies around for two or three weeks. Their outer casing, or exoskeleton, is still soft. Once it hardens up, the young scorpions can climb down and live on their own.

DO ANIMALS TEACH THEIR YOUNG?

Baby animals are born with some knowledge. They learn other skills by watching and copying.

Tamarins usually give birth to twins. Both parents teach the babies.

What do tamarins teach their young?

If an adult golden lion tamarin finds a tree hollow full of grubs, it doesn't just feed itself or even collect food for its young. It calls until the baby comes to see. The monkey teaches its offspring exactly how to catch a meal.

What instincts do young have?

Parent animals don't have to teach their babies what danger looks or smells like. Youngsters are born with this knowledge. They also seem to know whether it's best to hide, fight, or flee.

DO DUCKLINGS RECOGNIZE THEIR PARENTS?

When they hatch, ducklings follow the first moving thing they see!

Can ducklings swim after hatching?

When goslings and ducklings hatch, they are able to waddle and swim, and are programmed to follow their mother. This is called imprinting.

Who's the mother?

Imprinting is nature's way of making sure goslings and ducklings stick together and stay safe. If there is no mother around, the orphaned chicks might imprint on another animal or even a human.

A couple of days after hatching, goslings and ducklings can no longer imprint. If they see something larger than them, their reaction now is fear!

WHY ARE PUPPETS USED FOR FEEDING?

Puppets are used as pretend parents in breeding programs.

Which birds are fed this way?

Cranes are wetland birds. Siberian and whooping cranes are just two species in danger of dying out. When chicks are bred in captivity, they have more chance of survival—but they need to be able to fit in with a real flock when they're released.

Crane chick

In 1941, there were just 21 whooping cranes left in the wild. Today there are around 600 birds.

Who work the puppets?

Workers on breeding programs wear crane glove puppets when they feed the chicks. They want the chicks to keep their natural trust of cranes and fear of humans.

HOW DO MUSK OXEN PROTECT THEIR CALVES?

Musk oxen form walls around their young.

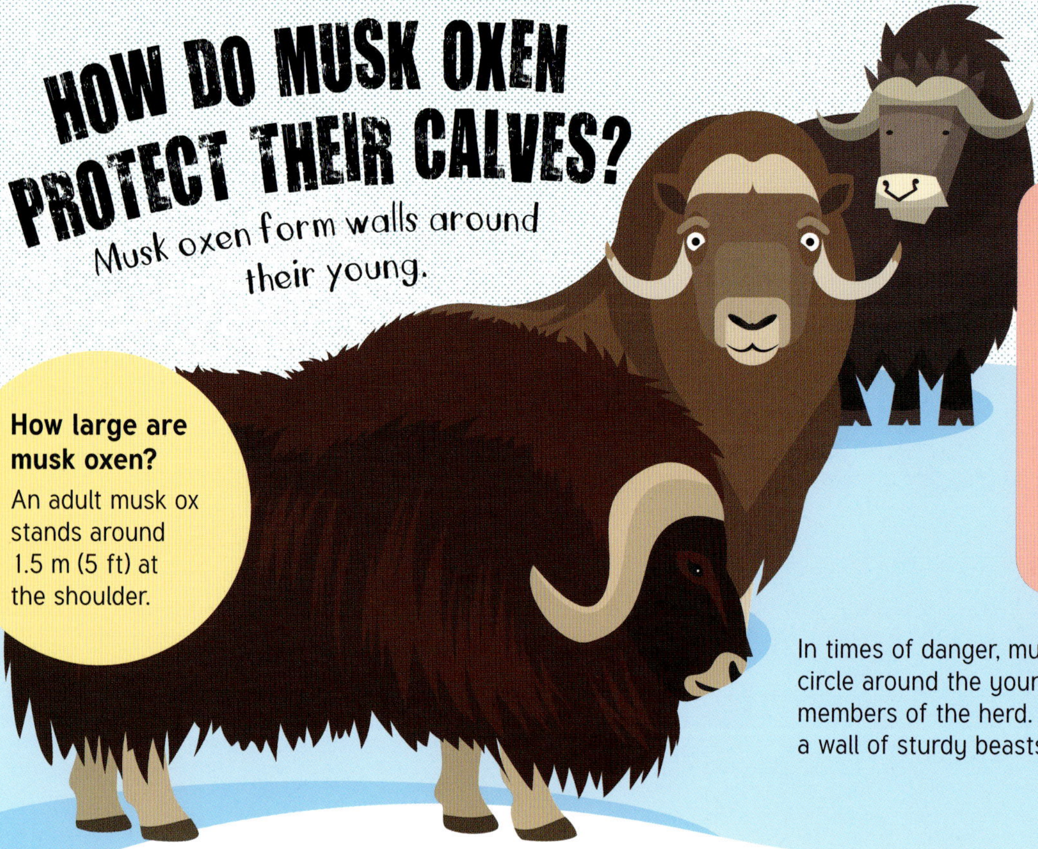

Where do musk oxen live?

Herds of musk oxen live in the Arctic. Wolves and other predators could attack their calves, especially when they are newborn. The herd works together to protect the young.

How large are musk oxen?

An adult musk ox stands around 1.5 m (5 ft) at the shoulder.

In times of danger, musk oxen form a defensive circle around the youngest, oldest, and weakest members of the herd. Any predator is faced by a wall of sturdy beasts with long, curved horns.

CAN WILDEBEEST RUN AT BIRTH?

Yes, wildebeest babies are born ready to run in minutes!

Why do the young have to run so soon?

Also known as gnus, wildebeest are large antelopes that live in herds on African grasslands. They're constantly on the move for fresh grazing. Their calves scramble to their feet within minutes of being born—if they don't, they'll be left behind.

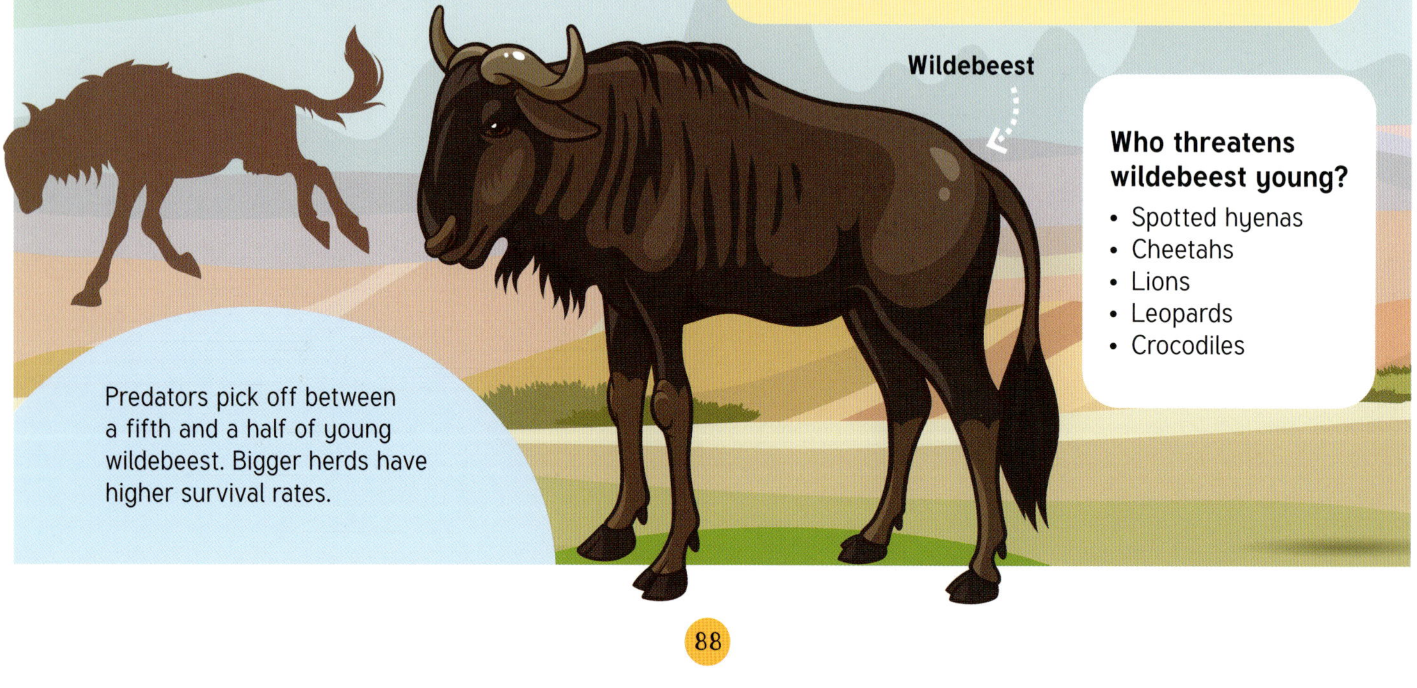

Who threatens wildebeest young?

- Spotted hyenas
- Cheetahs
- Lions
- Leopards
- Crocodiles

Predators pick off between a fifth and a half of young wildebeest. Bigger herds have higher survival rates.

DO ANIMALS DIE OF OLD AGE?

Yes. Just like humans, wild mammals become less able as they get older and eventually die.

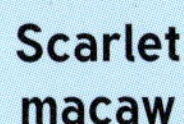

Macaws live for up to 80 years.

Scarlet macaw

Queen termite

African queen termites can live up to 60 years. During their lifetime, they lay around 200 million eggs.

Do animals live longer than 100 years?

On average, a giant tortoise reaches the age of 175, but there are stories of some that have lived longer than 250 years.

What is the oldest wild bird?

An albatross named Wisdom, tracked since 1956, is considered to be the oldest confirmed wild bird to have lived.

Albatross

A wormy parasite called *Loa loa* can live in the human eye for up to 15 years.

How long do koi carp live for?

These beautiful fish don't quite last for eternity, but they do live 225 years or more. No wonder people keep koi carp in temple pools.

Koi carp

Do any insects have long lives?

Most insects don't live longer than a year, but some wood-boring beetles live for 50 years.

A great white shark swims the seas for around 70 years.

Great white shark

The giant tubeworms that grow up around deep-sea vents can live for at least 170 years.

DO MAYFLIES ONLY LIVE FOR MINUTES?

A mayfly nymph lives for years, but its adult life lasts just days, hours, or even minutes.

Adult mayfly

There are more than 2,000 different mayfly species.

Mayfly nymph

How do mayflies develop?

The mayfly lays its eggs in fresh water. The larvae, or nymphs, eat algae for up to three years. When the mayfly finally comes out of the water, it leaves behind its old exoskeleton.

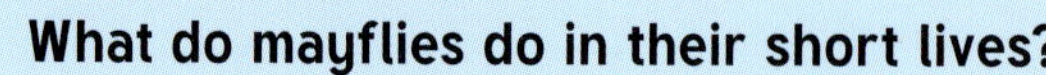

What do mayflies do in their short lives?

The mayfly's new, adult form has wings. The insect takes to the air, mates, and dies. If it's a female, it drops its eggs into the water first, and the cycle begins again.

CAN ANY ANIMALS LIVE FOREVER?

A few species of jellyfish are immortal —able to go on living forever!

How is this possible?

The immortal jellyfish has a neat trick that means it can live forever. If it's sick, old, or wounded, it turns back into a polyp. From here it buds into new larvae and grows into new medusas—on and on forever!

Immortal jellyfish

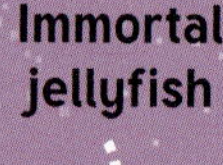

What is the jellyfish life cycle?

A jellyfish usually goes through five life stages—egg, planula, polyp, larva, and medusa (adult jellyfish). When medusas release sperm and eggs into the water, the life cycle starts again with each fertilized egg.

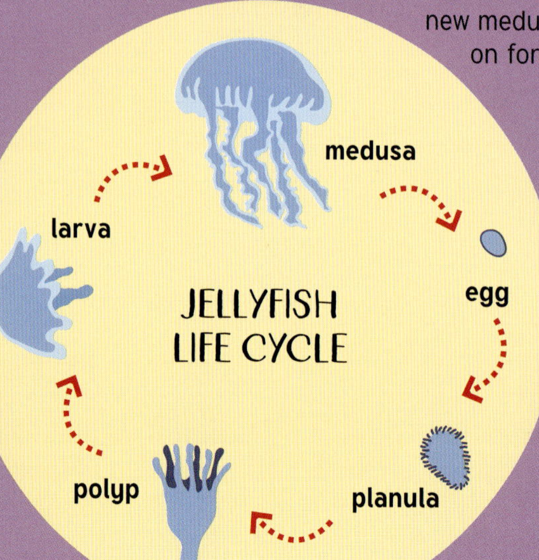

DO AXOLOTLS GROW UP?

Not fully. Most amphibians grow legs and move onto land, but not the axolotl.

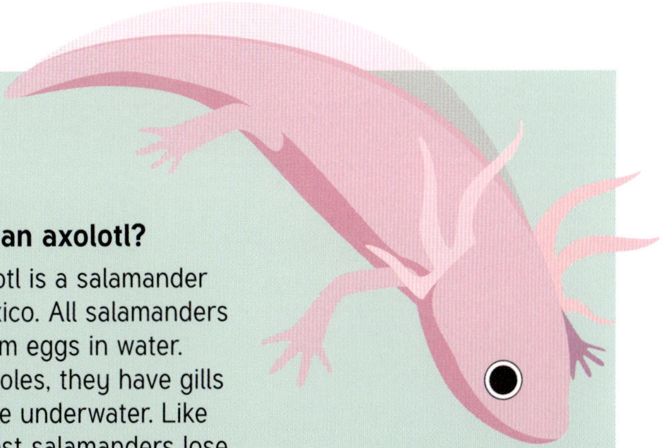

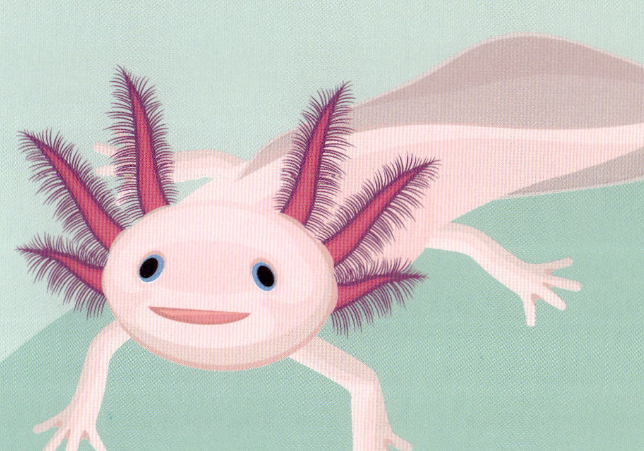

What is an axolotl?

The axolotl is a salamander from Mexico. All salamanders hatch from eggs in water. Like tadpoles, they have gills to breathe underwater. Like frogs, most salamanders lose their gills, develop lungs, and live on land as adults but not axolotls.

Most axolotls are mottled brown or black, but some are white, pink, or golden.

Where do axolotls live?

The axolotl lives its whole life in the water. It keeps its feathery gills and its tail fin and stays in its lake home. It feeds on worms, insect larvae, mollusks, and even fish.

DO CROCODILES SHED TEARS?

A crocodile's eyes produce moisture all the time, but they are not tears due to emotion.

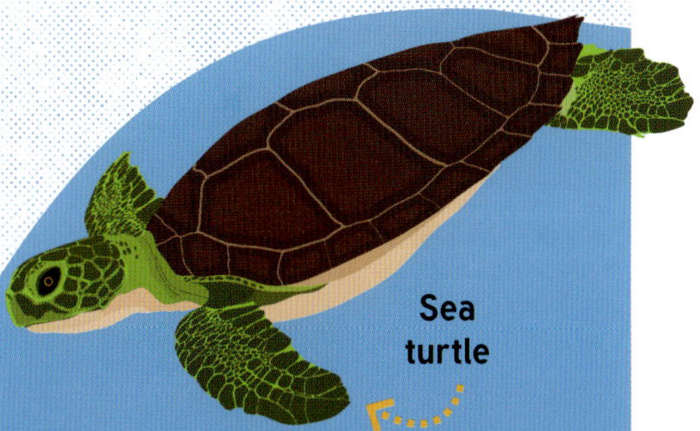

Sea turtle

Crocodile

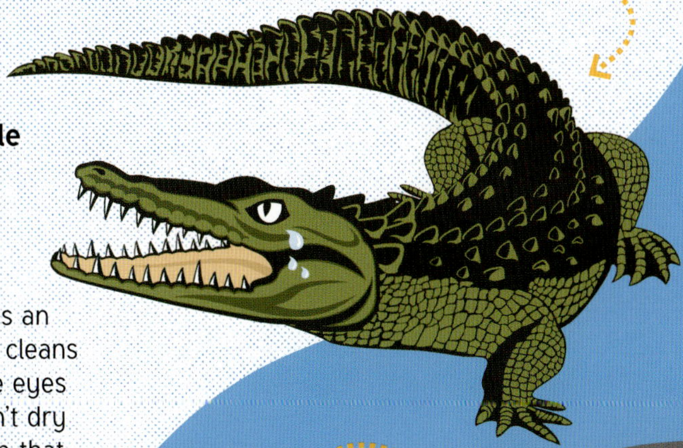

Is the crocodile feeling sad?

Fluid constantly flows from a crocodile's tear ducts and it does an important job. It cleans and protects the eyes so that they don't dry up. It's not a sign that the crocodile feels sorry for its victim!

Do turtles cry?

Sea turtles "cry" to get rid of some of the sea salt in their bodies. Their salt gland is near their eyes.

Sharks have salt glands in their bottoms!

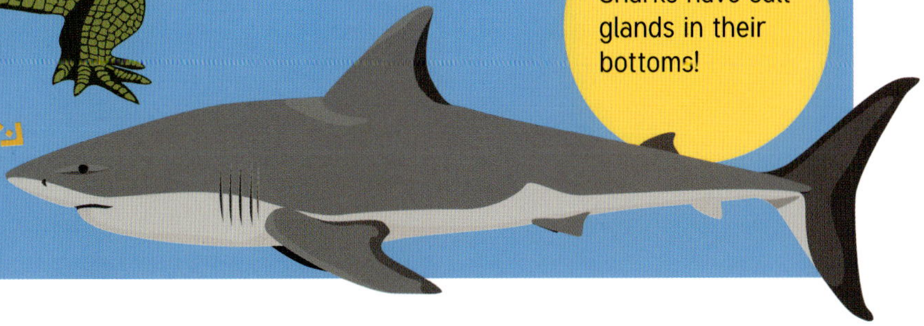

Great white shark

DO SNAKES HAVE BENDY BONES?

No, but snakes have lots and lots of bones which help to make them such flexible reptiles.

The longest snake is the reticulated python. It can grow to 7.6 m (25 ft) or more.

How are snakes so flexible?

Snakes are bendy and flexible because they have so many bones—400 or more, compared to just 206 in adult humans.

What's inside a snake?

The snake's throat makes up the front third of its body. The rest is mostly its stomach and digestive system.

How big are flying foxes?

The largest flying fox has a wingspan of around 1.8 m (6 ft).

ARE THE LARGEST BATS FOXES?

Flying foxes are the world's largest bats. They are named for their doglike faces, and are not actually related to foxes.

Do flying foxes use echoes to "see?"

Flying foxes live in tropical rain forests in Asia, Australasia, and East Africa. Unlike small bat species, they don't have sonar. They use sight and smell to find food—nectar, flowers, pollen, and fruit.

How heavy are flying foxes?

The Indian flying fox weighs up to 1.6 kg (3.5 lb)—the same as a small Chihuahua!

The smallest flying fox species weighs just 750 g (1.5 lb).

DOES A CAMEL'S HUMP STORE WATER?

No, humps help a camel to survive in the desert because they store fat.

How many humps?

Camels can turn the fat back into energy. Most camels are dromedaries, with one hump. Bactrian camels live in Central Asia and have two humps.

How do camels help humans?

Desert people have kept camels for 5,000 years. As well as being strong, hardy pack animals, they provide milk, meat, and hair for making textiles.

What makes camels desert-proof?

✓ Fatty hump
✓ Not losing much water as sweat or urine
✓ Double row of eyelashes to keep out sand
✓ Wide feet to spread their weight

WHAT ARE RHINO HORNS MADE OF?

Rhinoceros horns are made from keratin, just like your hair and fingernails.

How many horns?

White and black rhinos live in Africa and have two horns. Indian and Javan rhinos have one horn, just 55 cm (22 in). The rare Sumatran rhino has two, but one is very short and stubby.

Horns are a bit like EXTREMELY matted hair!

What was the longest rhino horn?

The longest rhino horn was 1.5 m (5 ft) long. It belonged to a white rhino.

During the Ice Age, herds of woolly rhinos roamed Europe and northern Asia.

WHERE DO HALF OF THE WORLD'S ANIMALS LIVE?

Tropical rain forests. They are excellent habitats, warm and wet, with lush plant life.

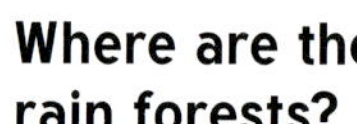
Scarlet macaw

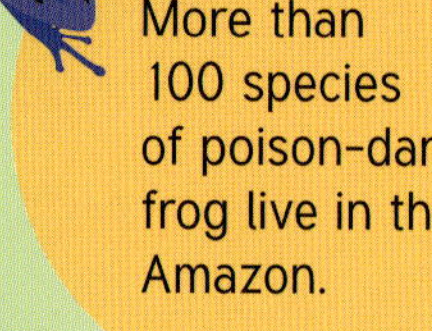
Poison-dart frog

Spider monkey

Who lives in the Amazon?
- 430+ mammal species
- 1,300 birds
- 400+ reptiles
- 400+ amphibians
- 3,000 fish

More than 100 species of poison-dart frog live in the Amazon.

Where are the rain forests?
Tropical rain forests grow near the equator, the imaginary line around the middle of the Earth. The Amazon in South America is the largest rain forest. It rains there nearly every day and the temperature is around 27 ˚C (80 ˚F).

Piranha

Green tree snake

DO SNAKES SHED THEIR SKIN?

All snakes, large and small, peel off their skin, leaving behind a ghostly shell.

Do snakes lose scales?

A snake's skin is made up of small, overlapping scales. Scales are tough, but after a few months' wear and tear they need replacing. The old skin splits to reveal a shiny new skin underneath!

Coral snake

Iguana

Iguanas and other lizards shed their skin in patches, not all in one piece like snakes.

Do turtles shed their skin?
Most turtles don't shed their skin. Instead, they grow a new layer under their shell.

Crocodile scales are tough and plate-like. They're replaced one at a time.

Crocodile

Turtle

ARE URBAN ANIMALS THE SMARTEST?

Urban animals need their wits about them. Some have bigger brains than their country cousins!

Gecko

House geckos keep insects under control by eating them. How helpful! However, they're also a nuisance because they poop everywhere!

Which carnivore is most common in towns?

The red fox is found in more places around the world than any other carnivore (meat-eater).

There are about a dozen species of fox. The red fox is the largest, and the most common in cities.

Which other animals have moved into towns?

Coyotes and raccoons scavenge and hunt across North America in many habitats, including towns and cities.

Red fox

Are town pigeons a problem?

Pigeons are small but deadly. They carry microbes such as salmonella, listeria, and cryptococcus, which causes a life-threatening form of meningitis.

There are 400 million rock pigeons in cities worldwide.

Macaque

Which animal has turned to thieving?

Macaques living in Southeast Asian countries have become skilled pickpockets!

Rock pigeon

Which creature caused millions of deaths?

Black rats spread the Black Death, or plague, through a flea they carried that killed up to 100 million people during the 1300s.

How many rats live in New York City?

The city has around two million rats, mostly brown ones.

Brown rat

DO GROUND SQUIRRELS CARRY PARASOLS?

Ground squirrels are rodents related to prairie dogs. They use their tails as sunshades!

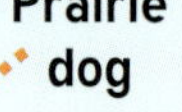

Another neat tail trick

1. A snake approaches.
2. The prairie dog waves its tail up and down as a warning.
3. The snake detects heat from the tail and thinks the prairie dog is bigger than it really is, so decides not to attack.

How useful are their tails?

All squirrels, including ground squirrels, can flick back their tail to shade their body. It lowers their temperature by up to 3 °C (5 °F)!

How big are prairie dog communities?

One prairie dog "town" in Texas was home to 400 million prairie dogs. It covered 65,000 sq km (25,000 sq miles).

WHO IS THE KING OF THE SWINGERS?

Out of all the primates, the gibbon is the best at swinging from branch to branch using only its arms.

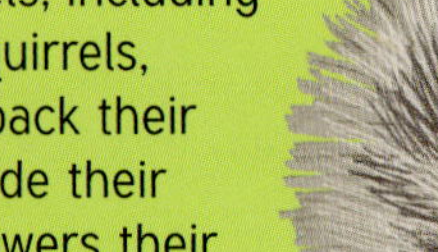

What makes a gibbon a great swinger?

Fast and agile, a gibbon can swing 15 m (50 ft) between branches at speeds up to 56.3 kph (35 mph). It has ball-and-socket wrist joints that rotate 360 degrees, long arms, long hands, and long, grasping fingers. The gibbon is also much smaller and lighter than any other ape.

Speed comes at a price! Most gibbons break a bone at least once in their life.